EXPECTANT LITTLE KNITS

Expectant Little Knits

Chic

Designs

for

Moms

to **Be**

SUZANNE J.E. TOURTILLOTT

LARK BOOKS

A Division of Sterling Publishing Co., Inc.
New York/London

Development Editor
SUZANNE J. E. TOURTILLOTT

Editor
DONNA DRUCHUNAS

Art Director
STACEY BUDGE

Cover Designer
CINDY LABREACHT

Photographer
STEWART O'SHIELDS

Library of Congress Cataloging-in-Publication Data

Tourtillott, Suzanne J. E.
  Expectant little knits : chic designs for moms to be / Suzanne J. E. Tourtillott.
      p. cm.
  Includes index.
  ISBN-13: 978-1-60059-151-8
  ISBN-10: 1-60059-151-5
  1. Knitting--Patterns. I. Title.
  TT820.T598 2007
  746.43'2041--dc22

                                     2007017614

10 9 8 7 6 5 4 3 2 1

First Edition

Published by Lark Books, A Division of
Sterling Publishing Co., Inc.
387 Park Avenue South, New York, N.Y. 10016

Distributed in Canada by Sterling Publishing,
c/o Canadian Manda Group, 165 Dufferin Street
Toronto, Ontario, Canada M6K 3H6

Distributed in the United Kingdom by GMC Distribution Services,
Castle Place, 166 High Street, Lewes, East Sussex, England BN7 1XU

Distributed in Australia by Capricorn Link (Australia) Pty Ltd.,
P.O. Box 704, Windsor, NSW 2756 Australia

If you have questions or comments about this book, please contact:
Lark Books
67 Broadway
Asheville, NC 28801
(828) 253-0467

Manufactured in China

ISBN 13: 978-1-60059-151-8
ISBN 10: 1-60059-151-5

For information about custom editions, special sales, premium and corporate purchases, please contact Sterling Special Sales Department at 800-805-5489 or specialsales@sterlingpub.com.

Contents

S ure, an impending baby brings a glow, a feeling of well-being like never before, but there's still the matter of dressing that bump. Wearing flattering knitwear during pregnancy makes perfect sense, but not until this collection have knitting moms-to-be—and their friends and family— been able to find such stylish designs. The knitted tops, skirts, dresses,

Knit for the Bump, Mama

and cover-ups presented here fit well and flatter the figure in ways that all modern, fashion-forward knitters want.

So there's no time to waste. *Expectant Little Knits* is for you! Whether you're a fashionista or a comfort-before-beauty mom-to-be (or mom-again), you'll find garments to suit your fancy in these pages, plus skill-building lessons to help you expand your knitting expertise.

"From Frumpy to Fabulous" on page 12 provides an overview of contemporary maternity fashions with a quick peek back to the trends and not-so-chic choices of yesteryear. After learning about the limited choices expectant moms had in the past, you'll appreciate the range of styles available to today's maternity knitter.

Newer knitters and those needing a refresher on beyond-basics techniques can refer to pages 115 through 126 for step-by-step instructions on knitting, finishing, and embellishment techniques. This chapter also covers the supplies and materials you'll need in your knitting bag before you get started.

The heart of *Expectant Little Knits* is the projects. In this collection of maternity garments, over a dozen talented designers have put their hands to the task of creating comfortable and stylish clothes that you'll be proud to wear throughout your pregnancy—and afterward. And there are projects for every skill level, too. Whether you've just learned to knit or you've been knitting for your whole life, you'll find projects here that engage your creativity.

The Comfy Camo Top on page 14 is a perfect beginner project for the casual, young or young-at-heart mother-to-be. The Day-to-Night Dress on page 46 is dolled up with sparkly beads for an elegant night on the town or a festive holiday party. And between those two extremes of comfort and couture, you'll find tank tops, dresses, cardigans, and pullovers in every style. Made with yummy wools, hemp, washable acrylic, and many other fibers, the projects in this book feature yarns in every price range.

Now pregnant women everywhere can look great while they're expecting. Get out those needles and cast on for a fashionable and flattering hand-knit maternity wardrobe!

BELLY BITS expectant —and beyond

Fashion's shapes are so eclectic these days that maternity styles range from snugly skintight to sweeping empire waistlines. And that means the knitted pieces in this book don't have to turn into instant giveaways the minute delivery is over. Cinch up the excess with a wide belt. Wear the bigger tops with skinny pants and ballet flats. It's all about attitude!

basics

HERE YOU'LL LEARN about the tools and materials you will need to create the beautiful garments in this book. The back of the book also includes instructions for working special stitches and techniques you may not be familiar with. If you're a new knitter, read this over before you begin. If you have a bit of knitting experience, check back here if you need a refresher or a lesson on an unfamiliar technique.

materials and tools

One of the most fun parts of knitting is shopping for the materials and tools that are used to create original and stylish garments. The following sections will give you some ideas on stocking your yarn stash and your toolkit.

YARN, FABULOUS YARN

Who can resist a shop full of gorgeous yarns in rainbow colors? The yarns available today are both beautiful and functional. There are many types of yarn on the market, and each has different properties, benefits, and drawbacks. A little thought will help you make selections that are best for your personal lifestyle.

PROTEIN FIBERS—such as wool, alpaca, and mohair—are easy to knit because they have natural stretch. These yarns knit up into springy fabrics that are warm in winter and cool in spring and fall. Most are too hot for summer wear.

PLANT FIBERS—such as cotton, linen, and bamboo—are less stretchy and often make stronger yarns. These fibers are a little more challenging to knit with than wool because they can be quite slippery.

SYNTHETICS—such as nylon, polyester, and acrylic—are man-made fibers. These fibers can be machine-washed and dried, and make very practical, hard-wearing items.

NOVELTY YARNS are usually made from man-made fibers or several different fibers blended or plied together in unusual textures and color combinations. They can be difficult to knit with because of their unusual textures, but these textures also help hide mistakes.

KNITTING NEEDLES

Knitting needles are the tools you'll use most often, so take the time to try different kinds and see what's most comfortable for you. Needles come in many shapes, sizes, and materials. Each type behaves differently. Here are some options to consider:

STRAIGHT NEEDLES are used for knitting garments that are made in separate pieces and sewn together. **CIRCULAR NEEDLES** are used for projects that are knitted in the round with no seams. These types of needles come in various lengths, so check the requirements in the pattern to be sure you purchase needles of the correct size and length. **DOUBLE-POINTED NEEDLES** are used for knitting small circular sections of garments, such as the cuffs on sweater sleeves that are knitted in the round. Double-pointed needles are also used for some special techniques such as I-cord.

For beginning knitters, **WOODEN** or **BAMBOO NEEDLES** are good choices because they aren't slippery, or "fast." The extra texture of these needles makes dropping stitches less frequent. After you've finished a few projects, you may want to try **PLASTIC** or **METAL** needles. These are "faster" than wood, but give slightly less control. Wood and plastic are warmer than metal needles, and you may find them more comfortable to the touch, especially in colder weather or if you have arthritis.

needle sizes

Metric sizes are the most accurate way to judge knitting needle sizes. U.S. needle sizes from different manufacturers may vary in actual measurements.

METRIC (MM)	U.S.
2	0
2.25	1
2.5	1
2.75	2
3	3
3.25	3
3.5	4
3.75	5
4	6
4.25	6
4.5	7
5	8
5.5	9
6	10
6.5	10½
7	10½
8	11
9	13
10	15
12	17
15	19
19	35
20	36
25	50

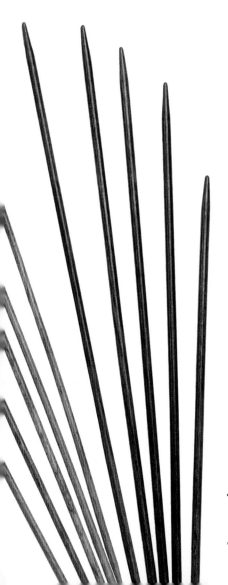

building a knitter's toolkit

After you've decided what types of knitting needles you like to work with, it's time to fill up the rest of your knitting toolkit. Here are some common notions and supplies that you'll find useful.

A SMALL TAPE MEASURE that fits in your knitting bag is essential for measuring gauge and making sure your garments are working up to the desired size.

A BLUNT TAPESTRY NEEDLE is used for weaving in ends and sewing seams.

SMALL SCISSORS or a yarn cutter are used to trim ends. If you travel a lot with your knitting, make sure to check with the airline to find out what types of cutting tools are allowed.

AN EMERY BOARD and **HAND CREAM** will help keep your fingers from catching on your knitting.

CROCHET HOOKS are useful for picking up dropped stitches. Buy an inexpensive set with multiple sizes so you have the right size on hand when you need to add a crochet edging or accent to your project.

ROW COUNTERS will help you keep your place in patterns and charts.

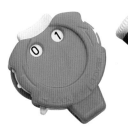

STITCH MARKERS are essential for keeping track of your work, and they also help stop you from losing your place when you're knitting a complicated lace or cable pattern.

NEEDLEPOINT PROTECTORS and plastic pins are also handy additions to your toolkit.

You should always make a **PHOTOCOPY OF YOUR PATTERN** and keep it, along with a **PENCIL**, in your knitting bag so you can make notes as you go. To build a useful reference guide after you finish your project, put the pattern into a journal, along with a yarn label, your gauge swatch, and a photo of the finished project. You'll find this handy in the future if you want to remake a garment from the same pattern, see what yarn or needles you used, or give help to a friend in designing something for her wardrobe.

keeping it all together

A KNITTING BAG large enough to hold your project—and with a pocket to hold small tools—is one of the most fun things to shop for. From a basic, recycled shopping bag to gorgeous tapestry totes, there are bags available for every taste and budget. Make sure the one you select is large enough to hold your project as it grows. When you start, you'll have just one ball of yarn, your needles, and your pattern. But when you're getting close to the finish line, you'll have an entire garment in your bag.

ZIPPER-LOCKING FREEZER BAGS and plastic pencil pouches help organize your tools and keep everything dry should a disaster happen. These can be slipped inside a larger knitting bag for easy access.

knitting abbreviations

Knitting patterns are often full of abbreviations intended to save space. This list will help you identify any abbreviations with which you're unfamiliar.

TERM	DEFINITION
"	inch(es)
*^	repeat instructions between * symbols as indicated
()	repeat instruction in parentheses as indicated
beg	begin(ning)
BO	bind off
cm	centimeter(s)
cn	cable needle
CO	cast on
circ	circular
dec	decrease
dpn(s)	double-pointed needle(s)
est	established
foll	follows
g	gram(s)
inc	increase
k or K	knit
k2tog	knit two stitches together as one

k3tog	knit three stitches together as one
kf/b	knit into the front and back of the same stitch, increasing one stitch
m	meter(s)
LH	left hand
m1 or M1L	make one left slanting: With the left needle inserted from front to back, pick up the bar between the stitches on the left and right needles. Knit into the back to twist the stitch.
M1R	make one right slanting: With the left needle inserted from back to front, pick up the bar between the stitches on the left and right needles. Knit into the front to twist the stitch.
meas	measures
oz	ounce
p or P	purl
p2tog	purl two stitches together as one
p2tog-tbl	purl two together through the back loops: Keeping the yarn in front, slip two stitches as if to knit, then place them back on the left needle. Purl these same two stitches together through the back loops.
patt	pattern
pm	place marker
psso	pass slip stitch over
rem	remain(ing)
rep	repeat(ing)

Rev St st	reverse stockinette stitch, reverse stocking stitch
RH	right hand
RS	right side
rnd(s)	round(s)
s2kp	slip two, knit one, pass slipped stitches over: Slip next two stitches as if to knit them together, knit next stitch, pass slipped stitches together over the stitch just knit.
sc	single crochet
sm	slip marker
ssk	slip, slip, knit: Slip the next two stitches one at a time to the right needle as if to knit. Insert the left needle into the front of the stitches and knit the two stitches together through the back loops.
sssk	slip, slip, slip, knit. Work as ssk but with three stitches.
sl	slip
st(s)	stitch(es)
St st	stockinette stitch, stocking stitch
tbl	through the back loop
tog	together
W&T	wrap and turn
wyif	with yarn in front
wyib	with yarn in back
WS	wrong side
yd	yard(s)
yo	yarn over

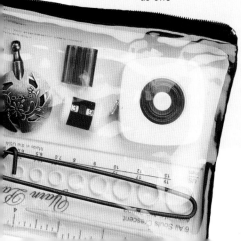

From Frumpy to Fabulous

Every morning, millions of pregnant women stand in front of their closets, wondering what to wear. In recent history, maternity-wear choices have been limited. In fact, before the 1930s, mass-market designs specifically for the pregnant woman didn't even exist! To make matters worse, history has never quite been able to make up its mind about pregnancy. Celebrate it or hide it? Revere it or revile it?

In the fourteenth century, pregnancy was actually very fashionable. Women wanted to emulate the Madonna, and young girls and women who weren't pregnant wore pillows stuffed under their dresses.

By the sixteenth century, the Farthingale, a metal cone contraption worn under the dress, had come into vogue. The Farthingale, accompanied by a tight bodice, camouflaged hips and thighs while ensuring a flat stomach.

Fortunately, Empress Josephine popularized the empire-waist dress during the French Revolution, freeing pregnant women everywhere to loosen up and breathe. During the Victorian Era, when modesty (but not, apparently, common sense) abounded, women were again constricted with the return of the corset and an emphasis on the wasp waist.

And so it goes—styles and fashion have fluctuated from the comfortable to the restrictive to the downright dangerous.

Mid-twentieth century, Lucille Ball's kicky capris and cute little smocks flattered her pregnant figure on TV. Jackie Kennedy, pregnant on the campaign trail with JFK in 1960, also inspired women with her classic A-line dresses, neat little coats, and matching pillbox hats and gloves.

Maternity clothing still had a ways to go in the '70s and '80s. Some still remember their few shapeless and, well, rather dumpy options, worn over and over and over again. Tent dresses with matronly bows, shapeless sacklike tops, and men's oversized shirts predominated. Pregnant women everywhere were crying out for comfy, sexy, and beautiful clothing options, and the fashion industry responded.

Today, mothers-to-be don't have to settle for frumpy, oversized anything. Clingy, hip, and funky clothing encourages women to take pride in their new, temporarily Rubenesque, figures. Maternity clothing has become a fun way to celebrate one of the most precious times in a woman's life.

SKILL LEVELS

Basic knitting skills are all that are required to make most of the projects in this book. Each project is identified with a skill level as defined below.

BEGINNER: These projects are appropriate for all knitters. If you know how to knit, purl, cast on, and bind off, you have the required skills.

EASY: These projects are for knitters who have made at least two or three small projects. They may include some shaping, multiple colors, or easy-stitch patterns.

INTERMEDIATE: These projects are appropriate for knitters who are confident in their experience. They include shaping, circular knitting, color work, or more intricate pattern stitches such as lace.

ADVANCED: These projects are for very experienced knitters. They include unusual shaping techniques and complex pattern stitches that require your full attention.

Ready to Knit?

Now that you've reviewed some of the fundamentals, you're ready to dive in and start knitting!

BELLY BITS I'm not big, I'm hot

Some women love the swelling belly and others can't wait to get back to fighting weight, but for those days when you've really had it with not being able to spot your own toes, rev up your fashion quota with fun accessories. Glam up that "pregnant outfit" with an oversized necklace, a lightweight narrow scarf-and-a-half, or some flashy suede platform shoes. Then murmur your due date to yourself, like a mantra.

Go commando with this babydoll-style top—a first-ever camouflage maternity piece! The ingenious design, comprised of rectangles, tubes, and trapezoids, make it a low-stress knitting adventure.

comfy camo top

DESIGN BY **LARA RUTH WARREN**

EXPERIENCE LEVEL EASY

SIZE S (M, L, XL)

FINISHED MEASUREMENTS

BUST: 27 (29, 31, 33)"/69 (74, 79, 84)cm, unstretched

SKIRT WIDTH: 39¼ (40½, 41¾, 43)"/100 (103, 106, 109)cm, ungathered

SKIRT LENGTH: 18 (18, 20, 22)"/46 (46, 51, 56)cm

✲ **NOTE:** Bust has negative ease and stretches to fit; skirt is gathered with extra room built in.

materials

APPROX TOTAL: 1140yd/1042m of worsted weight acrylic yarn:

COLOR A: 896yd/819m in black

COLOR B: 244yd/223m in camouflage

KNITTING NEEDLES: 4.5mm (size 7 U.S.) needles, *or size to obtain gauge for tube top*

6mm (size 10 U.S.) circular needle 29"/74cm long, *or size to obtain gauge for skirt*

8mm (size 11 U.S.) needles for sleeves

10yd/9m black elastic thread

4yd/3.6m black grosgrain ribbon ½"/13mm wide

Tapestry needle

gauge

TOP: 14 sts and 28 rows = 4"/10cm over Garter st using smallest needles

SKIRT: 14 sts and 20 rows = 4"/10cm over St st using medium needles

Always take time to check your gauge.

pattern stitches

STOCKINETTE STITCH (CIRCULAR)

ALL RNDS: Knit.

GARTER STITCH (BACK AND FORTH)

ALL ROWS: Knit.

instructions

TUBE TOP

Using smallest needles and B, CO 33 (35, 37, 39) sts.

Work Garter st until piece meas 27 (29, 31, 33)"/69 (74, 79, 84)cm.

BO. Sew short ends together to form a tube.

SKIRT

Using circular needles and color A, CO 157 (162, 167, 172) sts. Join to knit in the round, being careful not to twist sts.

Knit every rnd until piece meas approx 18 (18, 20, 22)"/ 46 (46, 51, 56)cm.

BO rem sts.

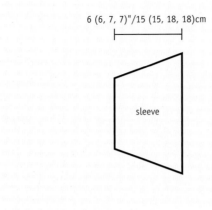

6 (6, 7, 7)"/15 (15, 18, 18)cm

sleeve

9½ (10, 10½, 11)"/24 (25, 27, 28)cm

tube top

27 (29, 31, 33)"/69 (74, 79, 84)cm

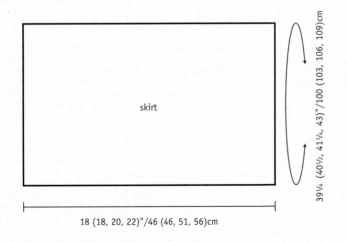

39¼ (40½, 41¾, 43)"/100 (103, 106, 109)cm

skirt

18 (18, 20, 22)"/46 (46, 51, 56)cm

SLEEVES (MAKE 2)

Using largest needles and color B, CO 14 sts.

ROW 1 (RS): *Sl 1, k1, yo, k2tog; rep from * to last 2 sts, sl 1, k1.

ROWS 2 AND 4 (WS): Sl 1, p across row to last st, yo, k1— 16 sts after row 4.

ROW 3: *Sl 1, ssk, yo; rep from *, to last 3 sts, sl 1, k2.

✳ **NOTE:** The row end will change on each repeat as the number of sts increases. When you do not have enough sts to work the full pat rep at the end of the row, knit the rem sts.

Repeat rows 1–4 another 8 (8, 10, 10) times—32 (32, 36, 36) sts.

Knit 1 row. BO.

FINISHING

Using two strands of black elastic thread held together, thread the elastic through the top of the Skirt. Gather the Skirt in until it is the same size as the Tube Top, then tie the elastic in a knot to secure. Bury the ends of the elastic in the knitting.

SEW SKIRT TO TUBE TOP:

Using two strands of black elastic thread held together, thread the elastic through the BO edge of each Sleeve. Sew the short ends of each Sleeve to the front and back of the Tube Top. Cut two strands of color A approx 6"/15cm longer than the curved edge of the Sleeve. Use the tapestry needle to weave a strand through the curved edge of the Sleeve to gather it in a little. Weave in the ends.

Weave the black grosgrain ribbon through the bottom of the Tube Top approx ½– 1"/1–2.5cm from the waist, and tie the ends of the ribbon in a bow.

THIS DRESS WAS MADE WITH

(A) 2 skeins of Red Heart's *Supersaver Solids*, 100% acrylic; 10oz/282g = 488yd/446m, Black

(B) 1 skein Red Heart's *Supersaver Prints*, 100% acrylic; 5oz/141g = 244yd/223m, Camouflage

This car coat is designed to be worn both during and after pregnancy, open or closed with a pretty brooch. Slim sleeves fall to ribbed bell cuffs, and the ribbed border forms both a shawl collar and a cutaway hem.

deauville car coat

DESIGN BY **A.L. DE SAUVETERRE**

EXPERIENCE LEVEL EASY

SIZE S (M, L, XL)

FINISHED MEASUREMENTS

BUST: 34 (38, 42, 46)"/
86 (97, 107, 117)cm

LENGTH: 40 (41, 41, 41)"/
102 (104, 104, 104)cm

materials

1800 (1900, 2000, 2100)yd/
1646 (1737, 1829, 1920)m
hand-painted, Aran-weight
cashmere yarn in dark brown

KNITTING NEEDLES: 5.5 mm
(size 9 U.S.) *or size to obtain
gauge*

5.5mm (size 9 U.S.) circular
needles 60"/152cm long

Tapestry needle for sewing seams

2 stitch markers or safety pins

Jeweled brooch

gauge

18 sts and 24 rows = 4"/10cm
over St st

*Always take time to check your
gauge.*

pattern stitches

SLIP STITCH RIB PATTERN

ROW 1 (RS): P2, *K1, sl1
purlwise, K1, p2; rep from
* to end.

ROW 2: K2, *P3, K2; rep from
* to end.

Rep rows 1 and 2 for pat.

STOCKINETTE STITCH

ROW 1 (RS): Knit.

ROW 2: Purl.

Rep rows 1 and 2 for pat.

instructions

✱ **TIP:** When using hand-painted yarn, for more even distribution of color, knit with two balls at a time, alternating between each ball every other row.

BACK

BOTTOM EDGE:

CO 34 (44, 52, 62) sts.

Work in St st, shaping as foll:

ROW 1 (RS): Knit.

ROW 2: CO 3 sts, work these 3 sts, then work the next st through the back loop, work to end.

ROWS 3–9: Rep row 2.

ROW 10: Purl.

ROW 11: Knit.

ROWS 12 AND 13: Rep row 2.

Rep rows 10 through 13 twice more—76 (86, 94, 104) sts.

Pm at each end of the piece. When joining seams, the bottom edges of the two front pieces will line up from these markers.

MAIN BODY

Work even in St st until piece meas 6"/15cm from bottom. End after completing a WS row.

Dec 1 st on each side, every 22 (16, 22, 22) rows 2 (3, 2, 2) times, then inc 1 st on each side, every 22 (16, 22, 22) rows 2 (3, 2, 2) times.

Work even until piece meas 18 (18½, 18½, 18½)"/46 (47, 47, 47)cm from markers. End after completing a WS row.

ARMHOLE SHAPING:

BO 2 (4, 5, 6) sts at beg of next 2 rows, then dec 1 st on each side, every other row 2 (3, 4, 6) times—68 (72, 76, 80) sts rem.

Work even until armhole meas 8 (8½, 8½, 9)"/20 (22, 22, 23)cm. End after completing a WS row.

SHOULDER SHAPING:

BO 5 (6, 6, 7) sts at beg of next 4 (6, 2, 4) rows, then BO 6 (0, 7, 8) sts at beg of next 2 (0, 4, 2) rows.

BO rem 36 sts.

RIGHT FRONT

CO 3 sts.

ROW 1 (RS): Inc 1, knit to end—4 sts.

ROW 2: Purl.

Working in St st, continue to inc 1 st at center front edge every other row 34 (39, 43, 48) more times. AT THE SAME TIME, when piece meas 6"/15cm from CO edge, dec 1 st on side edge every 22 (16, 22, 22) rows 2 (3, 2, 2) times, then inc 1 st on side edge, every 22 (16, 22, 22) rows 2 (3, 2, 2) times—38 (43, 47, 52) sts.

Work even until piece meas 15 (16, 16, 16½)"/38 (41, 41, 42)cm from markers. End after completing a WS row.

(RS) Beg with next row, dec 1 st at neck edge every other row until 16 (18, 20, 22) sts rem. AT THE SAME TIME, when piece meas same as back to armhole, beg armhole shaping on a WS row.

ARMHOLE SHAPING:

NEXT ROW (WS): BO 2 (4, 5, 6) sts at beg of row.

Dec 1 st at beg of row, every other row 2 (3, 4, 6) times.

Work even until armhole meas 8 (8½, 8½, 9)"/20 (22, 22, 23)cm. End after completing a RS row.

SHOULDER SHAPING:

BO 5 (6, 6, 7) sts at beg of next 2 (3, 1, 2) WS rows, then BO 6 (0, 7, 8) sts at beg of next 1 (0, 2, 1) WS rows.

LEFT FRONT

CO 3 sts.

ROW 1 (RS): Knit to last st, inc 1—4 sts.

ROW 2: Purl.

Working in St st, continue to inc 1 st at center front edge every other row 34 (39 43, 48) more times. AT THE SAME TIME, when piece meas 6"/15cm from cast on, dec 1 st on side edge every 22 (16, 22, 22) rows 2 (3, 2, 2) times, then inc 1 st on side edge, every 22 (16, 22, 22) rows 2 (3, 2, 2) times—38 (43, 47, 52) sts.

Work even until piece meas 15 (16, 16, 16½)"/38 (41, 41, 42)cm from markers. End after completing a WS row.

(RS) Beg with next row, dec 1 st at neck edge every other row until 16 (18, 20, 22) sts rem. AT THE SAME TIME, when piece meas same as back to armhole, beg armhole shaping on a RS row.

ARMHOLE SHAPING:

NEXT ROW (RS): BO 2 (4, 5, 6) sts at beg of row.

Dec 1 st at beg of row, every other row 2 (3, 4, 6) times.

Work even until armhole meas 8 (8½, 8½, 9)"/20 (22, 22, 23)cm. End after working a WS row.

SHOULDER SHAPING:

BO 5 (6, 6, 7) sts at beg of next 2 (3, 1, 2) RS rows, then BO 6 (0, 7, 8) sts at beg of next 1 (0, 2, 1) RS rows.

SLEEVES (MAKE 2)

CO 57 (57, 62, 62) sts.

Work in Slip Stitch Rib pat, and AT THE SAME TIME, dec 1 st on each side, every 2 (4, 4, 6) rows 1 (2, 2, 3) time(s), then dec 1 st on each side, every 4 (6, 6, 8) rows 6 (4, 3, 1) time(s)—43 (45, 52, 54) sts rem.

Work even until piece meas 10"/25cm, ending after completing a WS row.

CHANGE TO St st AND BEG SLEEVE SHAPING:

Inc 1 st every 6 (9, 9, 10) rows 4 (6, 5, 1) times, then every 8 (0, 0, 12) rows 3 (0, 0, 3) times—57 (57, 62, 62) sts.

Continue until piece meas 18 (19, 19, 19½)"/46 (48, 48, 50)cm from bottom.

BO 2 (4, 5, 6) sts at beg of next 2 rows, then dec 1 st on each side, every other row 2 (3, 4, 6) times—49 (43, 44, 38) sts rem.

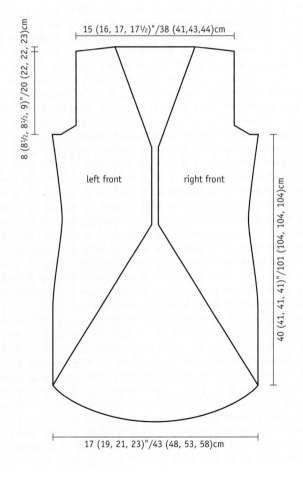

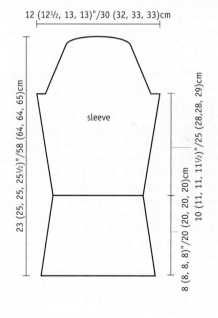

SIZE S ONLY: Dec 1 st on each side every row 6 times, then dec 1 st on each side every other row 5 times—27 sts rem.

SIZES M, L, XL ONLY: Dec 1 st on each side every 2 (2, 4) rows 8 (7, 4) times, then dec 1 st on each side every 4 rows 1 (1, 4) times—25 (28, 22) sts rem.

ALL SIZES: BO 3 sts at beg of next 4 rows, then BO rem 15 (13, 16, 10) sts.

FINISHING

Block all pieces. Sew shoulder seams, set in Sleeves, and sew side seams.

BAND:

With circular needle, pick up and knit stitches starting at center Back bottom hem and working along right side edge to right Front, up right Front neck edge to center Back neck. Make sure that the number of stitches picked up is a multiple of 5 + 2.

✳ **NOTE:** Take care to pick up and BO sts loosely to avoid puckering of the fabric along the hem and edges.

Work in Slip Stitch Rib pat until border meas 9"/23cm. BO loosely in rib.

Repeat for other side.

Sew ribbed border at center Back neck and center Bottom hem. Weave in ends. Block or steam press garment again as necessary. Secure sweater with brooch as desired.

THIS PROJECT WAS MADE WITH 18 (19, 20, 21) balls of A.L. de Sauveterre's *Pippin,* 100% cashmere, 1.75oz/50g = approx 100yd/91m per ball, color Chocolate

The side pleats on this easy-to-wear piece may look complicated, but once you've started working them, the simple logic of the pattern will make perfect sense.

goddess tank

DESIGN BY **CHER UNDERWOOD FORSBERG**

EXPERIENCE LEVEL
INTERMEDIATE

SIZE S (M, L, XL)

FINISHED MEASUREMENTS
34½ (38½, 42½, 47)"/
88 (98, 108, 119)cm

materials

990 (1210, 1430, 1650)yd/
905 (1106, 1308, 1509)m
cotton/modal blend sport-
weight yarn in tan

KNITTING NEEDLES: 3.75mm
(size 5 U.S.) circular needle
24"/61cm long, *or size to
obtain gauge*

3.75mm (size 5 U.S.) double-
pointed needles *or size to
obtain gauge*

Stitch markers

Stitch holders

gauge

23 sts and 35 rows =
4"/10cm over St st

*Always take time to check
your gauge.*

pattern stitches

STOCKINETTE STITCH

ROW 1 (RS): Knit.

ROW 2 (WS): Purl.

Rep rows 1 and 2 for pat.

K1, P1 RIBBING

ROW 1: (K1, p1) across. If
worked over an odd number
of sts, end k1.

ALL ROWS THEREAFTER:
Knit the knits and purl the
purls.

JOIN PLEAT (JP)

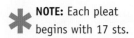 **NOTE:** Each pleat
begins with 17 sts.

Slip the next 6 sts to a dpn
(face of the pleat plus the
slip st), sl the following 6
sts to a second dpn (fold
line and turn-under of the
pleat). Turn the dpns so the
WS of the face and the
turn-under are together.

Slip 1 st from the pleat face
to the right needle. Knit the
first st from the turn-under
of the pleat, passing the
slipped st over it.

*Slip 1 st from the face to
the right needle, then 1
from the turn-under to the
right needle. Knit the first st
from the underside, and pass
the slipped sts over it one at
a time.* Rep from * to * 4
times—6 sts rem in pleat.

instructions

BACK

CO 110 (123, 136, 149) sts.

Work in K1, P1 Ribbing for
½ (½, ¾, ¾)"/1.3 (1.3, 2,
2)cm. End after completing
a WS row.

Change to St st and work
even until piece meas 1 (1¼,
1½, 1½)"/2.5 (3, 4, 4)cm
from beg.

BODY SHAPING:

Dec 1 st at each end of next
row, then every 20 (16, 16,
15) rows 4 (5, 5, 5) times—
100 (111, 124, 137) sts rem.

Work even until piece meas
12¾ (14, 14¼, 14½)"/32 (36,
36, 37)cm from beg. End after
completing a WS row.

ARMHOLE SHAPING:

BO 8 (9, 10, 9) sts at
beginning of next 2 rows. Dec
1 st at each end of every other
row 6 (8, 11, 16) times—
72 (77, 82, 87) sts rem.

Work even until armhole meas
8¼ (8½, 9, 9½)"/21 (22, 23,
24)cm. End after completing a
WS row.

NECK SHAPING:

Work both sides AT THE SAME
TIME. Work 22 (23, 24, 25)
sts, slip the next 28 (31, 34,
37) sts to a holder. Joining a
second ball of yarn, work rem
22 (23, 24, 25) sts. Dec 1 st at
neck edge every row 3 times—
19 (20, 21, 22) sts rem.

AT THE SAME TIME, when
armhole meas 8½ (8¾, 9½,
9¾)"/22 (22, 24, 25)cm, end
right shoulder after completing
a RS row and end left shoulder
after completing a WS row.
Shape shoulders as foll:

RIGHT SHOULDER:

NEXT ROW (WS): P14 (15, 15,
16) sts, W&T.

NEXT ROW (AND REM RS

ROWS): K to end.

NEXT WS ROW: P9 (10, 10, 10)
sts, W&T.

NEXT WS ROW: K to end.

NEXT WS ROW: P4 (5, 5, 5) sts,
W&T.

NEXT WS ROW: K to end.

NEXT WS ROW: P across all sts,
picking up wraps and working
them with the stitch they are
wrapped around as you come
to them. Slip sts to a holder.

LEFT SHOULDER:

NEXT ROW (RS): K14 (15, 15,
16) sts, W&T.

**NEXT ROW (AND REMAINING
WS ROWS):** P to end.

NEXT RS ROW: K9 (10, 10, 10)
sts, W&T.

NEXT RS ROW: K4 (5, 5, 5) sts,
W&T.

NEXT RS ROW: K across all sts,
picking up wraps and working
them with the st they are
wrapped around as you come
to them. Slip sts to a holder.

FRONT

CO 176 (189, 202, 215) sts.

Work in K1, P1 Ribbing for ½ (½, ¾, ¾)"/1.3 (1.3, 2, 2)cm. End after completing a WS row.

NEXT ROW (RS): K15 (16, 16, 16), pm, (k5, sl 1, k5, p1, k5) 3 times, pm, k44 (55, 68, 81) sts, pm, (k5, p1, k5, sl 1, k5) 3 times, pm, k15 (16, 16, 16).

NEXT ROW (WS): Purl.

Rep these two rows, working shaping as given for back, until piece measures 12¾ (14, 14¼, 14½)"/32 (36, 36, 37)cm from beg. End after completing a WS row.

NEXT ROW (RS): K10, JP 3 times, k44 (55, 68, 81) sts; JP 3 times, folding in the opposite direction, k10—100 (111, 124, 137) sts rem.

Work 1 WS row, then work 2 rows of armhole shaping as for Back—84 (93, 104, 119) sts.

Continue to shape armholes as for Back, and AT THE SAME TIME, beg neck shaping.

NECK SHAPING:

Work both sides AT THE SAME TIME. Work 39 (44, 49, 57) sts; join a second ball of yarn and BO next 6 (5, 6, 5) sts, work 39 (44, 49, 57) sts.

While continuing with armhole shaping as for Back, dec 1 st at neck edge of next row, then every 4 rows 1 (7, 8, 12) times, then every 5 rows 12 (8, 8, 6) times—19 (20, 21, 22) sts rem.

Shape shoulders as for Back.

FINISHING

Sew side seams to underarms. Using Kitchener stitch, graft Front and Back tog at shoulder seams.

NECKLINE:

With dpns pick up 132 (138, 152, 160) sts evenly around the neck. Join to work in the round. Work K1, P1 Ribbing for ½"/1.3cm. BO loosely.

ARMHOLES:

With dpns, pick up and K112 (116, 122, 128) sts around the armhole. Join to work in the round. Work K1, P1 Ribbing for ½"/1.3cm. BO loosely.

Weave in ends. Block sweater.

THIS SWEATER WAS MADE WITH 9 (11, 13, 15) skeins of Knit Picks' *Shine Sport*, 60% pima cotton/40% modal, 1.75oz/50g = 110 yd/101m per skein, color #23816 Willow

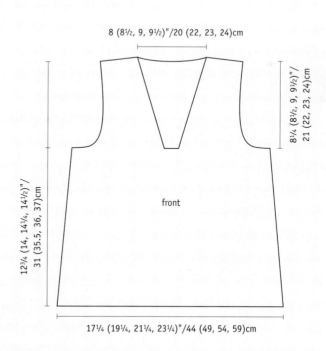

8 (8½, 9, 9½)"/20 (22, 23, 24)cm

8¼ (8½, 9, 9½)"/ 21 (22, 23, 24)cm

12¾ (14, 14¼, 14½)"/ 31 (35.5, 36, 37)cm

front

17¼ (19¼, 21¼, 23¼)"/44 (49, 54, 59)cm

This soft, stylish top is perfect for any new mom. Pearl buttons on each side open for easy nursing, and the resulting flap can be used as a light cover for a bit of privacy. When nursing days are over, seam up the sides and wear it as a regular sweater!

alpaca cable pullover

DESIGN BY **CHRISSY GARDINER**

EXPERIENCE LEVEL
INTERMEDIATE

SIZE S (M, L, XL)

FINISHED MEASUREMENTS

BUST: 36 (40, 44, 48)"/ 91 (102, 112, 122)cm

LENGTH: 22 (23, 24, 25)"/ 56 (58, 61, 64)cm

materials

1210 (1320, 1540, 1650)yd/1106 (1207, 1408, 1509)m 100% baby alpaca light-weight yarn in pink

KNITTING NEEDLES: 4mm (size 6 U.S.) *or size to obtain gauge*

Cable needle

Stitch holder

Tapestry needle for seaming and weaving in ends

Six pearl buttons, ³/₈"/10mm in diameter

gauge

20 sts and 28 rows = 4"/10cm in St st

22 sts and 32 rows = 4"/10 cm in Cable Wing st

Always take time to check your gauge.

pattern stitches

GARTER STITCH

Knit every st in every row.

STOCKINETTE STITCH

ROW 1 (RS): Knit.

ROW 2: Purl.

Rep rows 1 and 2 for pat.

instructions

BACK

CO 100 (110, 120, 130) sts.

Work in Garter st for ½"/1.3cm, slipping the 1st st of each row.

NEXT ROW (RS): Sl1, k to end.

NEXT ROW (WS): Sl1, k1, p to last 2 sts, k2.

Rep these 2 rows until piece meas 13 (13½, 14, 14½)"/ 33 (34, 36, 37)cm from beg. End after completing a WS row.

ARMHOLE SHAPING:

BO 13 (13, 14, 15) sts at beg of next 2 rows—74 (84, 92, 100) sts rem.

Work even in St st until armholes meas 9 (9½, 10, 10½)"/23 (24, 25, 27)cm. End after completing a WS row.

NEXT ROW (RS): BO 22 (26, 28, 32) sts, k30 (32, 36, 36), BO rem 22 (26, 28, 32) sts.

Break yarn and place rem 30 (32, 36, 36) sts on st holder for Back neck.

FRONT

CO 102 (114, 126, 138) sts.

Work in Garter st for ½"/1.3cm, slipping the first st of each row.

NEXT ROW (RS): Sl1, k1, work Cable Wing pat to last 2 sts, k2.

NEXT ROW (WS): Sl1, k1, work Cable Wing pat to last 2 sts, k2.

Rep these two rows until piece meas 3½"/9cm from beg, ending with row 6 of Cable Wing pat.

On the next row, substitute the foll buttonhole row for row 1 of Cable Wing pat (Chart A):

Buttonhole row (RS): Sl1, k1, k2tog, yo, k to last 4 sts, yo, ssk, k2.

*Cont working in Cable Wing pat for 3 (3, 3¾, 3¾)"/8 (8, 10, 10)cm from buttonhole row, ending with row 6 of Cable Wing pat. Rep buttonhole row in place of row 1 of Cable Wing chart. Rep from * once more (3 buttonholes on each side of Front).

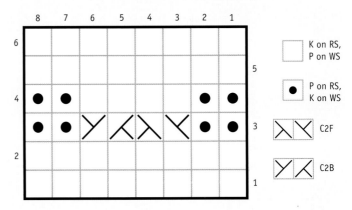

CHART A—CABLE WING PATTERN

	K on RS, P on WS
●	P on RS, K on WS
	C2F
	C2B

THIS PROJECT WAS MADE WITH 12 (13, 15, 16) balls of Blue Sky Alpaca's 100% alpaca, light weight, 1.75oz/50g = 110yd/100m per ball, color #516 Petal Pink

Work even in Cable Wing pat as est until Front meas approx 13 (13½, 14, 14½)"/33 (34, 36, 37)cm from beg. End after completing a WS row.

ARMHOLE SHAPING:

BO 8 (8, 9, 11) sts at beg of next 2 rows—86 (98, 108, 116) sts rem.

Cont working Cable Wing pat as est until armholes meas ½ (½, ¾, 1)"/1.3 (1.3, 2, 2.5) cm. End after completing a WS row.

DIVIDE FOR V-NECK:

NEXT ROW (RS): Work across first 43 (49, 54, 58) sts in pat as est. Place rem 43 (49, 54, 58) sts on st holder to be worked later.

NEXT ROW (WS): Work back across to left armhole edge.

UPPER LEFT FRONT

ROW 1 (RS): K1, work in Cable Wing pat as est to last 3 sts, k2tog, k1.

ROW 2: P2, work in Cable Wing pat as est to last st, p1.

Rep these 2 rows 20 (22, 25, 25) more times—22 (26, 28, 32) sts rem.

Work even in pat until armhole meas 9 (9½, 10, 10½)"/23 (24, 25, 27)cm. End after completing a WS row. BO all sts.

UPPER RIGHT FRONT

Place 43 (49, 54, 58) sts from st holder back onto needle and rejoin yarn at neck edge with RS facing.

ROW 1 (RS): K1, ssk, work in Cable Wing pat as est to last st, k1.

ROW 2: P1, work in Cable Wing pat as est to last 2 sts, p2.

Rep these 2 rows 20 (22, 25, 25) more times—22 (26, 28, 32) sts rem.

Work even in pat until armhole meas 9 (9½, 10, 10½)"/ 23 (24, 25, 27)cm. End after completing a WS row. BO all sts.

SLEEVES (MAKE 2)

CO 48 (50, 50, 52) sts.

Work in Garter st for ½"/1.3cm.

Change to St st and inc each side of Sleeve every 4 rows 21 (23, 25, 26) times—90 (96, 100, 104) sts.

Work even until Sleeve meas 18"/46cm from bottom edge. BO all sts.

FINISHING

Block pieces to finished measurements.

Sew shoulder seams. Sew Sleeve top edge to Front and Back armhole edges. Sew top of Sleeve edge to bound-off bottom edge of Front and Back armholes, overlapping the Front armhole bottom edge over the Back by 1"/2.5cm. Sew Sleeve seams.

Sew buttons to Back sides under buttonholes.

NECKBAND:

Place 30 (32, 36, 36) sts from Back neck holder onto needle and knit across them. Working down Left Front neck edge,

pick up and knit 3 sts for every 4 rows, pm, pick up one st in center point of V, pm. Working up Right Front neck edge, pick up the same number of sts as for Left Front.

NEXT RND: Purl.

NEXT RND: K to 2 sts before marker, ssk, k st between markers, k2tog, k to end of rnd.

Rep previous 2 rnds until neckband meas ½"/1.3cm. BO all sts.

Weave in ends.

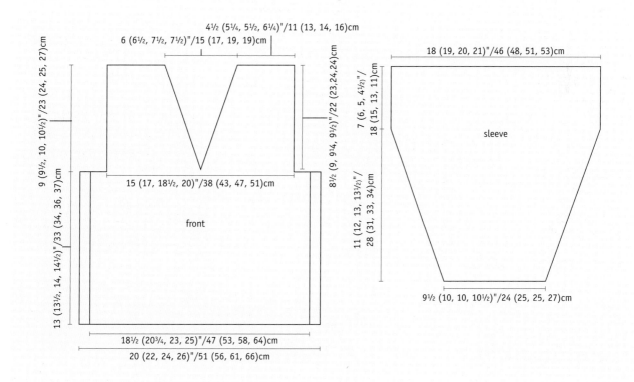

This simple summer cardi is for gals who like big needles! Using lightweight, braided yarn, you can knit this breezy summer cover-up in a long weekend.

wisteria lane cardigan

DESIGN BY **KATE BUCHANAN**

instructions

This sweater is made in pieces and sewn together after the knitting is complete. All pieces are made in Reverse Stockinette stitch.

BACK

CO 32 (34, 36, 38, 40, 42) sts.

Knit 4 rows.

Starting with a WS row, begin working in Rev St st. Work 2 (2, 2, 4, 4, 4) rows even, ending after completing a RS row.

WAIST SHAPING:

Dec 1 st at each end of next row and following 6th row once—28 (30, 32, 34, 36, 38) sts rem.

Work 3 rows even.

Inc 1 st at each end of next row, then every 16 (16, 16, 8, 8, 8) rows 1 (1, 1, 1, 2, 2) times—

30 (32, 34, 38, 40, 42) sts.

Work even until Back meas 12"/31cm from CO edge, ending after completing a RS row.

ARMHOLE SHAPING:

BO 2 (2, 2, 3, 3, 3) sts at beg of next 2 rows—26 (28, 30, 32, 34, 36) sts rem.

Work even until armhole meas 7 (7, 9, 9, 9¾, 9¾)"/18 (18, 23, 23, 25, 25)cm, ending after completing a WS row.

SHOULDER SHAPING:

NEXT ROW (RS): P10 (10, 12, 12, 13, 13), turn, leaving rem sts unworked on the needle.

NEXT ROW: Dec 1, knit to end of row—9 (9, 11, 11, 12, 12) sts in shoulder. Cut yarn.

NEXT ROW (WS): Join yarn on other end of row and k10 (10, 12, 12, 13, 13), turn.

EXPERIENCE LEVEL EASY

SIZE XS (S, M, L, XL, XXL)

FINISHED MEASUREMENTS

BUST: 32 (34, 36, 38, 40, 42)"/ 81 (86, 91, 97, 102, 107)cm

LENGTH: 19¼ (19¼, 21¼, 21¼, 22, 22)"/49 (49, 54, 54, 56, 56)cm

✳ NOTE: This fabric is very stretchy so don't be put off if the finished measurements seem tight.

materials

276 (322, 368, 368, 414, 460)yd/252 (294, 336, 336, 379, 421)m bulky cotton braid yarn in lavender

KNITTING NEEDLES: 12.75mm (size 17 U.S.) circular needles, 32"/81cm long *or size to obtain gauge*

Matching cotton thread

Sewing needle

2 buttons approx ⅞"/23mm in diameter

gauge

8 sts and 12 rows = 4"/10cm over Rev St st

Always take time to check your gauge.

pattern stitch

REV STOCKINETTE STITCH

ROW 1 (WS): Knit.

ROW 2 (RS): Purl.

Rep rows 1 and 2 for pat.

NEXT ROW: Dec 1, purl to end of row—9 (9, 11, 11, 12, 12) sts in shoulder.

BO all sts loosely.

RIGHT FRONT

CO 16 (17, 18, 19, 20, 21) sts.

Knit 4 rows.

Starting with a WS row, begin working in Rev St st. Work 2 (2, 2, 4, 4, 4) rows even, ending after completing a RS row.

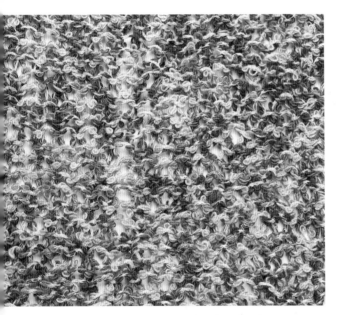

WAIST SHAPING:

(WS) Dec 1 st at beg of next row and following 6th row once—14 (15, 16, 17, 18, 19) sts rem.

Work 3 rows even.

Inc 1 st at beg of next row, then every 16 (16, 16, 8, 8, 8) rows 1 (1, 1, 2, 2, 2) times—16 (17, 18, 20, 21, 22) sts.

Work even until Front meas 12"/31cm from CO edge, ending after completing a RS row.

ARMHOLE SHAPING:

NEXT ROW (WS): BO 2 (2, 2, 3, 3, 3) sts at beg of row—14 (15, 16, 17, 18, 19) sts rem.

NECKLINE SHAPING:

(RS) Dec 1 st at beg of next row, then every 4 rows 4 (5, 4, 5, 5, 6) times—9 (9, 11, 11, 12, 12) sts rem.

Work even until armhole meas same as Back. BO.

LEFT FRONT

CO 16 (17, 18, 19, 20, 21) sts.

Knit 4 rows.

Starting with a WS row, begin working in Rev St st. Work 2 (2, 2, 4, 4, 4) rows even, ending after completing a RS row.

WAIST SHAPING:

(WS) Dec 1 st at end of next row and following 6th row once—14 (15, 16, 17, 18, 19) sts rem.

Work 3 rows even.

Inc 1 st at end of next row, then every 16 (16, 16, 9, 9, 9) rows 1 (1, 1, 2, 2, 2) times—16 (17, 18, 20, 21, 22) sts rem.

Work even until Front meas 12"/31cm from CO edge, ending after completing a WS row.

SHAPE ARMHOLES:

NEXT ROW (RS): BO 2 (2, 2, 3, 3, 3) sts at beg of row—14 (15, 16, 17, 18, 19) sts rem.

NECKLINE SHAPING:

(WS) Dec 1 st at beg of next row, then every 4 rows 4 (5, 4, 5, 5, 6) times—9 (9, 11, 11, 12, 12) sts rem.

Work even until armhole meas same as Back. BO.

SLEEVES (MAKE 2)

CO 18 (19, 20, 21, 22, 23) sts.

Knit 4 rows.

NEXT ROW (WS): Starting with a knit row, begin working in Rev St st.

Inc 1 st at beg and end every 3 rows 4 times, then inc 1 st at beg and end every 4 rows 4 (4, 4, 4, 5, 5) times—34 (35, 36, 37, 40, 41) sts.

Work even until sleeve meas 11¾ (11¾, 11¾, 12½, 12½, 12½)"/30 (30, 30, 32, 32, 32)cm from CO edge, or desired length. BO.

FINISHING

Using cotton thread and sewing needle, join seams as foll: Lay Fronts and Back with RS tog and gently pull pieces into shape. Backstitch along the shoulder seams by sewing through the top strand of each knitted loop. Lay body RS down and match up Sleeves to armholes. Backstitch in place.

Join side seams and Sleeve seams using backstitch. Turn garment RS out.

EDGING:

Beg at bottom corner of Left Front, pick up 1 st for every row along the front edge, 10 sts across Back neckline, and 1 st for every row along front edge of right edge.

Knit 1 row.

BO loosely as foll: K2tog, *slip st from right-hand needle to left-hand needle, k2tog; rep from * to end.

Weave in ends.

Using the photo as a guide, sew the buttons to the Left Front. The fabric is stretchy enough that you can push the button through without knitting a buttonhole.

THIS PROJECT WAS MADE WITH 6 (7, 8, 8, 9, 10) balls of Rowan's *Cotton Braid*, 68% cotton/22% viscose/10% linen, 1.75oz/50g = 46yd/50m per ball, color #362 Botticelli

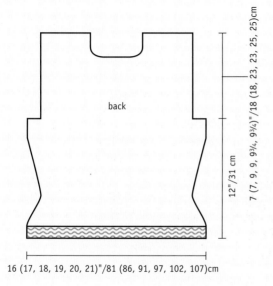

back

7 (7, 9, 9, 9¾, 9¾)"/18 (18, 23, 23, 25, 25)cm

12"/31 cm

16 (17, 18, 19, 20, 21)"/81 (86, 91, 97, 102, 107)cm

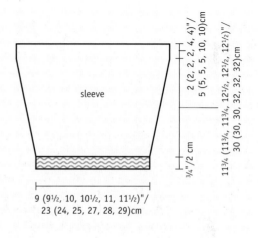

sleeve

2 (2, 2, 2, 4, 4)"/5 (5, 5, 5, 10, 10)cm

11¾ (11¾, 11¾, 12½, 12½, 12½)"/30 (30, 30, 32, 32, 32)cm

¾"/2 cm

9 (9½, 10, 10½, 11, 11½)"/23 (24, 25, 27, 28, 29)cm

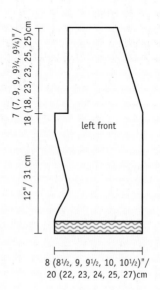

left front

7 (7, 9, 9, 9¾, 9¾)"/18 (18, 23, 23, 25, 25)cm

12"/31 cm

8 (8½, 9, 9½, 10, 10½)"/20 (22, 23, 24, 25, 27)cm

This sweater serves double duty. A well-placed button panel makes this sweater perfect for nursing. With optional belly-shaping, it can also be worn during pregnancy.

cowl-neck nursing sweater

DESIGN BY **SAUNIELL N. CONNALLY**

EXPERIENCE LEVEL
INTERMEDIATE

SIZE S (M, L, XL)

FINISHED MEASUREMENTS

BUST: 36 (39, 41, 45)"/91 (99, 104, 114)cm

LENGTH: 24½ (25½, 27, 28¼)"/62 (65, 69, 72)cm

materials

880 (990, 1100, 1320)yd/ 805 (905, 1006, 1207)m bulky weight 100% wool yarn

KNITTING NEEDLES: 5.5mm (size 9 U.S.) straight needles and circular needle 16"/41cm long, *or size to obtain gauge*

4.5mm (size 7 U.S.) circular needle 16"/41cm long *or size to obtain gauge*

6 buttons, ⅝"/1.6cm in diameter

gauge

14 sts and 22 rows = 4"/10cm over St st using larger needles

Always take time to check your gauge.

pattern stitches

SEED STITCH

Worked over an even number of sts.

ROW 1 (RS): *K1, p1, repeat from * to the end.

ROW 2 (WS): *P1, k1, repeat from * to the end.

Rep rows 1 and 2 for pattern.

STOCKINETTE STITCH (BACK AND FORTH)

ROW 1 (RS): Knit.

ROW 2 (WS): Purl.

Rep rows 1 and 2 for pattern.

STOCKINETTE STITCH (CIRCULAR)

ALL RNDS: Knit.

instructions

BACK

Using the larger straight needles, CO 68 (74, 78, 82) sts.

Work in Seed st for 8 rows, then change to St st.

When piece meas 9 (10,10, 11)"/23 (25, 25, 28)cm, dec 1 st at each end of next row as foll: k2, ssk, work to last 4 sts, k2tog, k2.

Repeat decs every 16 (8, 8,16) rows 1 (2, 2, 1) times— 64 (68, 72, 78) sts. **

Work even until piece meas 16½ (17½, 18½, 19½)"/ 42 (45, 47, 50)cm. End after completing WS row.

ARMHOLE SHAPING:

BO 4 sts at beg of next 2 rows.

NEXT ROW (RS): K2, s2kp, work to last 4 sts, k3tog, k1.

Work WS row even.

NEXT ROW (RS): K2, ssk, work to last 4 sts, k2tog, k1.

Repeat decs every RS row 4 times—42 (46, 50, 56) sts.

When armhole meas 7½ (8½, 9, 9)"/19 (22, 23, 23)cm, BO 10 (11, 13, 15) sts at beg of next 2 rows. Place rem 22 (24, 24, 26) sts on holder.

FRONT BOTTOM

Work the same as for Back to **—64 (68, 72, 78) sts. On next RS row, beg short row belly shaping.

*SHORT ROW 1 (SR1): Knit to last 4 sts, W&T, work to last 6 sts, W&T.

SHORT ROW 2 (SR2): Knit to 4 sts before last wrapped st, W&T, work to 4 sts before last wrapped st, W&T.

Repeat SR2 4 more times for a total of 12 wrapped sts. After turning, with RS facing, knit to end picking up wrapped stitches. Break yarn, and with RS facing, join yarn at beg of row. Work RS row, picking up remainder of wrapped sts. Work 1 WS row even.

NOTE: Short row belly-shaping adds 2"/5cm in length at center front. Rep short row once more for a larger belly.

Work even for 2 (2, 4, 4) rows.

Knit 6 rows. BO all sts.

FRONT TOP

Using larger straight needles, CO 64 (68, 72, 78) sts.

Work in Seed st for 3 rows, then change to St st.

WORK BUTTONHOLES:

NEXT ROW (WS, SIZES S, M, L ONLY): Work 6 (8, 10) sts, k2tog, yo, *work 8 sts, k2tog, yo, rep from * 4 times, work to end.

NEXT ROW (WS, SIZE XL ONLY): Work 10 sts, *k2tog, yo, k9, k2tog, yo, k9, k2tog, yo, work 10 sts, and rep from * once.

ALL SIZES: Work 2 rows of Seed st, then work 10 (10, 14, 14) rows of St st.

ARMHOLE SHAPING:

Work armholes the same as for Back until armhole meas 4 (4¾, 5½, 5½)"/10 (12, 14, 14)cm—42 (46, 50, 56) sts.

NEXT ROW (RS): Work 13 (14, 16, 18) sts, BO center 16 (18, 18, 20) sts, work to the end.

Attaching a 2nd ball of yarn and working sides separately, at next RS row dec 1 st at the neckline edge 3 times—10 (11, 13, 15) sts rem in each shoulder.

Work even until armhole meas 7½ (8½, 9, 9)"/19 (22, 23, 23)cm. BO.

SLEEVES (MAKE 2)

Using larger straight needles, CO 38 (38, 42, 42) sts.

Work in Seed st for 8 rows, then change to St st and work 24 rows.

NEXT ROW (RS): K2, inc 1 st, work to last 2 sts, inc 1, k2.

Rep inc every 10 (8, 8, 8) rows 4 6, 7, 7) more times—48 (52, 58, 58) sts.

Work even until Sleeve meas 17 (18, 19, 19)"/43 (46, 48, 48)cm.

CAP SHAPING:

BO 4 sts at beg of next 2 rows, then BO 3 sts at beg of next 2 rows.

NEXT ROW (RS): K2, ssk, work to last 4 sts, k2tog, k2.

Rep decs every 4 rows 4 more times—34 (38, 44, 44) sts, then rep decs every RS row 4 times—16 (20, 26, 26) sts.

BO rem sts.

FINISHING

Wash and block pieces to measurements. Sew shoulder seams. Set in Sleeves. Sew buttons on Front Bottom to correspond to buttonholes on Front Top. Button pieces together to form one Front. Sew side seams and Sleeve seams. Weave in ends.

COWL NECK:

Using smaller circular needle, and with RS facing, pick up 38 (46, 48,50) sts around Front neck, pm, pick up 22 (24, 24, 26) sts along Back, pm, and join to work in the round—60 (70, 72, 76) sts.

Turn piece inside out, and work even in St st for 3"/8cm.

Change to larger circular needle and work even until cowl meas 8"/20cm.

Work 8 rnds in Seed st, and BO loosely. Turn down collar so knit side is facing out.

Weave in ends.

THIS PROJECT WAS MADE WITH 8 (9, 10, 12) balls of Lana Grossa's *Royal Tweed,* 100% merino wool, 1.75oz/50g = 110yd/101m, color #25

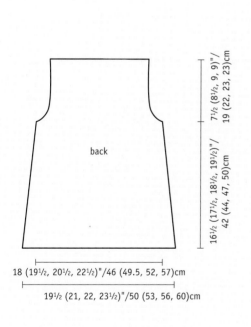

back

18 (19½, 20½, 22½)"/46 (49.5, 52, 57)cm

19½ (21, 22, 23½)"/50 (53, 56, 60)cm

16½ (17½, 18½, 19½)"/ 42 (44, 47, 50)cm

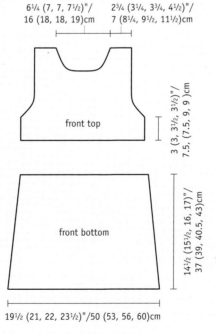

6¼ (7, 7, 7½)"/ 16 (18, 18, 19)cm

2¾ (3¼, 3¾, 4½)"/ 7 (8¼, 9½, 11½)cm

front top

3 (3, 3½, 3½)"/ 7.5, (7.5, 9, 9)cm

front bottom

14½ (15½, 16, 17)"/ 37 (39, 40.5, 43)cm

19½ (21, 22, 23½)"/50 (53, 56, 60)cm

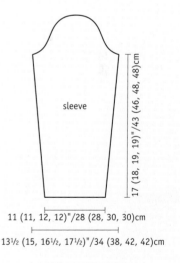

sleeve

17 (18, 19, 19)"/43 (46, 48, 48)cm

11 (11, 12, 12)"/28 (28, 30, 30)cm

13½ (15, 16½, 17½)"/34 (38, 42, 42)cm

front-finished lengths
Side seam-Armhole-to-hem
16½ (17½, 18½, 19½)"/42 (44, 47, 50)cm

Center belly-Armhole-to-hem
18½ (19½, 20½, 21½)"/47 (50, 52, 54.5)cm

This sleeveless top is worked in the round to the armholes. Made in a lustrous red wool/silk blend, it's dressy enough for that special holiday party. To accentuate the empire silhouette, especially in the later stages of pregnancy, try the optional twisted-cord belt.

double wing top

DESIGN BY **ANGELA HAHN**

EXPERIENCE LEVEL ADVANCED

SIZES S (M, L, XL)

FINISHED MEASUREMENTS

BUST: 32 (36, 41, 45)"/81 (91, 104, 114)cm

LENGTH: 24 (24½, 26, 26½)"/61 (62, 66, 67)cm

✳ **NOTE:** This top was designed to have minimal to slightly negative ease at and just under the bust. Bust measurements listed are for A cup. Additional width is added for B–C, C–D, and D–DD cups with short row shaping.

materials

750 (825, 950, 1050)yd/ 686 (754, 869, 960)m of wool/silk blend DK weight yarn in red; for A cup. Additional yardage is required for B–C, C–D, and D–DD cups.

KNITTING NEEDLES: 3.75mm (size 5 U.S.) circular needle 29– 42"/74–107cm long (needle should be slightly shorter than finished bust measurement) or size to obtain gauge

3.75mm (size 5 U.S.), 1 pair straight needles or 2nd circular needle

Stitch markers

Stitch holders or waste yarn

Tapestry needle for sewing seams and weaving in ends

gauge

24 sts and 32 rows = 4"/10cm in Double Wing Solid pat (Chart A), blocked

22 sts and 30 rows = 4"/10cm over St st, blocked

Always take time to check your gauge.

special stitch

DOUBLE INC

Lift running thread from front and k into back and front to inc 2 sts at once.

instructions

LOWER BODY

With circular needle, CO 240 (256, 288, 320) sts. Join to work in the round, being careful not to twist sts.

Set up Chart A pat as foll:

RND 1: Place beg of round marker, k120 (128, 144, 160) sts for Front, place mid-round marker, k120 (128, 144, 160) sts for Back.

RND 2: Work row 2 of Chart A 15 (16, 18, 20) times around.

Cont working Chart A until rows 1–10 of chart have been completed twice, then work rows 1–10 of Chart B 8 (8, 9, 9) times. Body should measure approx 12 (12, 13¼, 13¼)"/ 31 (31, 34, 34)cm.

EMPIRE WAIST SHAPING:

SIZE S ONLY: Work rows 1–10 of Chart C as foll: On row 1, k4, place left side marker, work to mid-round marker, k4, place right side marker, work to end—72 Front sts and 78 Back sts, 150 sts total.

SIZES M, L, AND XL ONLY: Work rows 1–10 of Chart D— 88 (99, 110) Front sts and 88 (99, 110) Back sts, 176 (198, 220) sts total.

ALL SIZES: Knit 3 rnds even.

INCREASE ROUND:

SIZE S ONLY: Remove beg of round marker, k to left side marker, inc 20 sts evenly across Front, remove mid-round marker; inc 8 sts evenly spaced across Back—92 Front sts and 86 Back sts, 178 sts total.

SIZES M, L, AND XL ONLY: Knit around, inc 16 (17, 20) sts evenly spaced across Front; inc 8 (9, 10) sts evenly spaced across Back—104 (116, 130) Front sts and 96 (108, 120) Back sts.

ALL SIZES: K3 (3, 4, 4) rounds.

CUP SHAPING:

Bra cup size will likely increase one to three sizes during pregnancy, so choose your number of short row reps not only based on pre-pregnancy cup size, but also based on how form-fitting you would like the top to be during pregnancy.

FOR A CUP: Skip to "Upper Body."

FOR B–C, C–D, AND D–DD CUP: Knit to 3 sts before right side marker, W&T, purl to 3 sts before left side marker, W&T. *K to 3 sts before last wrapped st, W&T, purl to 3 sts before last wrapped st, W&T. Rep from * until a total of 12 sts have been wrapped (6 on each side); RS of work should be facing you. Rep short rows once for a B–C cup, twice for a C–D cup, and 3 times for a D–DD cup.

UPPER BODY

Resume working in the round, picking up each wrap as you reach it and knitting it together with wrapped stitch.

Work even in St st until a total of 12 (14, 14, 14) rnds have been completed after increase round, placing a center front marker halfway between the side markers on the first round.

✳ **NOTE:** If you worked short rows, count the rounds on the Back.

For a proper fit, the top edge of the Double Wing pat must sit comfortably below the bust. Try on the sweater while wearing a bra. When the top edge of the garment is held up so it is a couple of inches (a few cm) below underarm level, the top edge should reach approx the level of the mid-breast. If the top of the Double Wing pat is not resting comfortably under the bust, work additional rnds as needed.

LEFT FRONT

Slip the Left Front sts onto the straight needles or 2nd circular needle. Leave rem sts on original circular needle.

ROW 1 (RS): Remove left side marker, k3, p1, ssk, k to 6 sts before center front marker, k2tog, p1, k3, remove center front marker.

ROW 2: P3, k1, p to 6 sts before end, p2tog tbl, k1, p3.

ROW 3: K3, p1, ssk, k to 4 sts before end, p1, k3.

ROW 4: P3, k1, p2tog, p to 6 sts before end, p2tog tbl, k1, p3.

Continue to dec 1 st at armhole edge every row 4 (6, 8, 12) more times. AT THE SAME TIME, cont to dec 1 st at neck edge every 3 rows (note that this will occur alternately on RS and WS rows). Once armhole decs have been completed, work even at armhole edge, continue to dec at neck edge every 3 rows until 18 (21, 24, 26) sts rem.

LEFT SHOULDER SHAPING:

When 18 (21, 24, 26) sts rem, on next WS row, work 9 (10, 12, 13) sts, W&T, on RS, work to end.

NEXT ROW (WS): Work across all sts, picking up and purling wrap tog with wrapped st, and working dec at neck edge as above.

Break yarn, leaving long tail to sew shoulder seam, and place rem 17 (20, 23, 25) sts on holder.

RIGHT FRONT

Slip the Right Front sts onto the straight needles or 2nd circular needle. Leave rem sts on original circular needle. With RS facing, join yarn at center front.

ROW 1 (RS): K3, p1, ssk, k to 6 sts before right side marker, k2tog, p1, k3, remove right side marker.

ROW 2: P3, k1, p2tog, p to 4 sts before end, k1, p3.

ROW 3: K3, p1, k to 6 sts before end, k2tog, p1, k3.

ROW 4: P3, k1, p2tog, p to 6 sts before end, p2tog tbl, k1, p3.

Continue to dec 1 st at armhole edge every row 4 (6, 8, 12) times more. AT THE SAME TIME, cont to dec 1 st at neck edge every 3 rows (note that this will occur alternately on RS and WS rows). Once armhole decs have been completed, work even at armhole edge, continue to dec at neck edge every 3 rows until 19 (22, 25, 27) sts rem.

RIGHT SHOULDER SHAPING:

NEXT ROW (RS): Work dec at neck edge as directed, then work to 10 (11, 13, 14) sts before end, W&T.

NEXT ROW (WS): Work to end.

NEXT ROW (RS): Work across all sts, picking up and knitting wrap tog with wrapped st.

NEXT ROW (WS): Work across all sts, working dec at neck edge as above.

Break yarn, leaving long tail to sew shoulder seam, and place rem 17 (20, 23, 25) sts on holder.

UPPER BACK

With RS facing, join yarn to Back.

ROW 1 (RS): K3, p1, ssk, k to 6 sts before end, k2tog, p1, k3.

ROW 2 (WS): P3, k1, p2tog, p to 6 sts before end, p2tog tbl, k1, p3.

Rep these 2 rows 3 (4, 5, 7) more times—70 (76, 84, 88) sts rem.

Work even in pat as est, for 28 (30, 30, 34) rows from start of armhole shaping; during one row, place center back marker at midpoint of Back.

RIGHT BACK

ROW 1 (RS): K3, p1, k to 6 sts before center back marker, k2tog, p1, k3. Remove center back marker.

ROW 2 (WS): P3, k1, p to 4 sts before end, k1, p3.

ROW 3 (RS): K3, p1, k to 6 sts before end, k2tog, p1, k3.

Rep rows 2 and 3 until 18 (21, 24, 26) sts rem. End after completing a RS row.

RIGHT BACK SHOULDER SHAPING:

NEXT ROW (WS): Work to 9 (10, 12, 13) sts before end, W&T.

NEXT ROW (RS): Work to end, including dec at neck edge.

NEXT ROW (WS): Work across all sts, picking up and purling wrap tog with wrapped st.

Break yarn and place rem 17 (20, 23, 25) sts on holder.

LEFT BACK

Join yarn to RS at center back.

ROW 1 (RS): K3, p1, ssk, k to 4 sts before end, p1, k3.

ROW 2 (WS): P3, k1, p to 4 sts before end, k1, p3.

Rep rows 1 and 2 until 19 (22, 25, 27) sts rem. End after completing a WS row.

LEFT BACK SHOULDER SHAPING:

NEXT ROW (RS): K3, p1, ssk, work to 10 (11, 13, 14) sts before end, W&T.

NEXT ROW (WS): Work to end.

NEXT ROW (RS): K3, p1, ssk, work across all sts, picking up and knitting wrap tog with wrapped st.

Work 1 more row, then break

yarn and place rem 17 (20, 23, 25) sts on holder.

FINISHING

Turn garment inside out so right sides of Front and Back are facing each other. Using sts held from front for one shoulder and the facing sts from back, join shoulder using the three-needle bind off. Repeat on 2nd shoulder.

Weave in all ends and block to measurements.

TWISTED-CORD BELT:

Cut 3 lengths of yarn, each approx 12'/4m long and make a twisted cord for a belt. To wear, tie the belt comfortably under the bust, at the top edge of the Double Wing section.

THIS PROJECT WAS MADE WITH 3 (4, 4, 5) skeins of Sundara Yarn's *DK Silky Merino*, 50% silk/50% merino wool, 3.5oz/100g = 250 yd/229m per skein, color #012

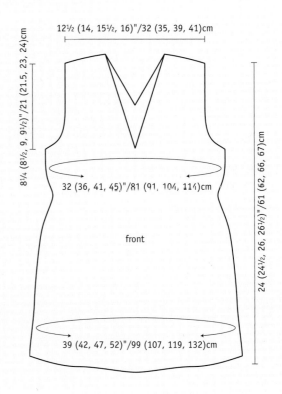

12½ (14, 15½, 16)"/32 (35, 39, 41)cm

8¼ (8½, 9, 9½)"/21 (21.5, 23, 24)cm

24 (24½, 26, 26½)"/61 (62, 66, 67)cm

32 (36, 41, 45)"/81 (91, 104, 114)cm

front

39 (42, 47, 52)"/99 (107, 119, 132)cm

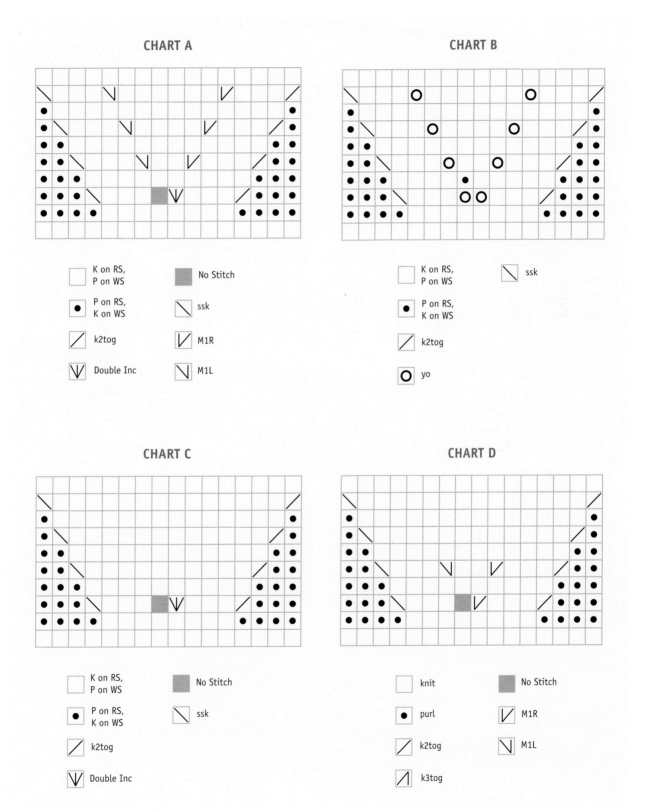

CHART A

CHART B

K on RS, P on WS	No Stitch
P on RS, K on WS	ssk
k2tog	M1R
Double Inc	M1L

K on RS, P on WS	ssk
P on RS, K on WS	
k2tog	
yo	

CHART C

CHART D

K on RS, P on WS	No Stitch
P on RS, K on WS	ssk
k2tog	
Double Inc	

knit	No Stitch
purl	M1R
k2tog	M1L
k3tog	

Put a positive spin on "pear-shaped" with this empire-waist top, perfect for before, during, and after pregnancy. The fabric is gently gathered with decreases below the bust and with increases in the bust area for a flattering shape.

anjou sleeveless top

DESIGN BY **ANGELA HAHN**

EXPERIENCE LEVEL

INTERMEDIATE

SIZE S (M, L, XL)

FINISHED MEASUREMENTS

BUST: 33 (36, 41, 45)"/84 (91, 104, 114)cm

UNDER BUST (MEASURED AT BRA BAND): 28 (32, 36, 40)"/71 (81, 91, 102)cm

LENGTH: 23 (24, 25, 25 ½)"/ 58 (61, 64, 65)cm

✱ **NOTE:** This top was designed to have minimal to slightly negative ease at and just under the bust.

materials

850 (925, 1025, 1125)yd/ 777 (846, 937, 1029)m of cotton or cotton blend light worsted weight yarn in light green

KNITTING NEEDLES: 4mm (size 6 U.S.) straight needles and circular needle 36–42"/91– 107cm long *or size to obtain gauge*

3.5mm (size 4 U.S.) circular needle 36–42"/91–107cm long *or size to obtain gauge*

3.5mm (size 4 U.S.) circular needle 16–20"/41–51cm OR set of double-pointed needles

✱ **NOTE:** Long circular needles should be slightly shorter than finished bust measurement.

Third needle of similar size for three-needle bind off

Stitch markers

Stitch holders or waste yarn (optional)

Tapestry needle

gauges

23 sts and 29 rows = 4"/10cm over Twist Stitch pat on larger needles, blocked

20 sts and 26 rows = 4"/10cm over Baby Cable Rib on smaller needles, blocked

Always take time to check your gauge.

pattern stitches

RIGHT TWIST (RT)

(Worked over 2 sts)

Skip first st on LH needle and knit 2nd st, then k first st and drop both sts from LH needle.

TWIST STITCH PATTERN (CIRCULAR)

(Worked over a multiple of 4 sts)

RND 1 (TWIST RND): *K1, RT, k1. Rep from * to end of rnd.

RNDS 2–4: Knit.

RND 5 (TWIST RND): K1, *k2, RT. Rep from * to last stitch, RT (working twist using last st of this rnd and first st of next rnd).

RNDS 6–8: Knit.

Rep rnds 1–8 for pattern.

TWIST STITCH PATTERN (BACK AND FORTH)

(Worked over a multiple of 4 sts)

ROW 1 (TWIST RND, RS): *K1, RT, k1. Rep from * to end of rnd.

ROW 2 (AND ALL WS ROWS): Purl.

ROW 3: Knit.

ROW 5 (TWIST RND): K1, *k2, RT. Rep from * to last stitch, RT (working twist using last st of this rnd and first st of next rnd).

ROW 7: Knit.

Rep rows 1–8 for pat.

BABY CABLE RIB PATTERN

(Worked over a multiple of 3 sts)

RND 1: *K2, p1. Rep from * to end of rnd.

RND 2: *RT, p1; rep from * to end of rnd.

RNDS 3–5: *K2, p1; rep from * to end of rnd.

RNDS 6–9: Rep rnds 2–5.

RND 10: *RT, k1; rep from * to end of rnd.

Rep rnds 1–10 for pat.

instructions

BODY

With larger, long circular needle, CO 216 (240, 264, 300) sts.

SET UP RND: Join, place right side marker, k108 (120, 132, 150) sts for Back, place left side marker, k108 (120, 132, 150) sts for Front.

Work even in Twist Stitch pat until 23 (24, 25, 26) twist rnds have been completed; body should meas approx 13 (13½, 14, 14½)"/33 (34, 36, 37)cm from CO edge.

Work 1 more rnd.

DEC RND: Change to smaller, long circular needle. *K2tog, k1; rep from * to end of rnd—144 (160, 176, 200) sts.

Work rnd 1 of Baby Cable Rib pat, and AT THE SAME TIME, inc 0 (1, 1, 1) st immediately after right side marker and inc 0 (1, 0 0) st immediately after left side marker, working incs into rib pat—144 (162, 177, 201) sts.

Work rnds 2–10 of Baby Cable Rib pat.

Knit one rnd.

INCREASE RND: Inc 12 (15, 19, 19) sts evenly spaced across 72 (81, 89, 101) Back sts— 84 (96, 108, 120) sts in Back, then:

FOR SIZE S ONLY: K3, (inc 1, k2) 15 times, inc 1, k6, (inc1, k2) 16 times, k3—104 sts in Front.

FOR SIZE M ONLY: K2, inc 1, k6, (inc 1, k2) 13 times, inc 1, k6, inc 1, k6, (inc, k2) 13 times, inc 1, k6, inc 1, k3— 112 sts in Front.

FOR SIZE L ONLY: K3, (inc 1, k2) 19 times, inc 1, k6, (inc 1, k2) 20 times, k3—128 sts in Front.

FOR SIZE XL ONLY: KI4, (inc 1, k3) 3 times, (inc 1, k2) 14 times, (inc 1, k3) 2 times, inc 1, k6, (inc 1, k3) 2 times, (inc 1, k2) 14 times, (inc 1, k3) 3 times, inc 1, k4—140 sts in Front.

After inc rnd, you should have 188 (208, 236, 260) sts total.

Knit 1 rnd then change to Twist Stitch pat. Work until 5 (5, 6, 6) twist rnds have been completed.

For a proper fit, the Baby Cable Rib band must sit comfortably below the bust. Try on the sweater. When the top edge of the garment is held up to slightly below the underarm level, the top edge should just cover the top of the bust, and the band should rest below the bust. If the band is riding too high, work additional rnds, ending after working a twist rnd.

Knit 1 more rnd, stopping 5 (6, 7, 8) sts before end of rnd.

DIVIDE FOR FRONT AND BACK:

Continue in Twist Stitch pat as est (if RT falls within 2 sts of edge, knit those sts instead). AT THE SAME TIME, bind off next 10 (12, 14, 16) sts, work across Back sts until 5 (6, 7, 8) sts before left side marker, BO next 10 (12, 14, 16) sts.

LEFT FRONT

Work across the next 39 (41, 46, 50) sts, turn.

✱ **NOTE:** Leave the rest of the body sts on the needle while working only the Left Front sts, or place rem sts on hold.

NEXT ROW (WS): BO 3 sts, p to end.

NEXT ROW (RS TWIST ROW): K1, k2tog, work to end.

NEXT ROW: BO 2 (2, 3, 3) sts, p to end.

Cont to dec 1 st at armhole edge every RS row 4 (5, 6, 7) more times, and AT THE SAME TIME, dec 1 st at neck edge every row 6 (6, 8, 8) times, then every RS row 5 (5, 4, 6) times, then every 4 rows 5 (5, 5, 4) times—13 (14, 16, 18) sts rem in left shoulder.

✱ **NOTE:** For neck edge, decs on RS rows, work to last 2 sts, ssk; on WS rows, p2tog-tbl, work to end.

Work even until 12 (13, 14, 14) twist rows have been completed above underarm

bind off and top meas approx 22 (23, 24, 24½)"/56 (58, 61, 62)cm.

SHAPE SHOULDER USING SHORT ROWS:

On 2nd WS row after twist st row, p6 (7, 8, 9), W&T, on RS work to end.

NEXT ROW (WS): Work across all sts, picking up wrap.

Place sts on holder.

RIGHT FRONT

Place center 16 (18, 22, 24) Front sts on holder. Join yarn to RS of rem 39 (41, 46, 50) Front sts.

NEXT ROW (RS): BO 3 sts, work to last 3 sts, ssk, k1.

NEXT ROW (WS): Purl.

NEXT ROW (TWIST ROW): BO 2 (2, 3, 3) sts, work to 2 sts before end, dec 1 as above.

NEXT ROW: Purl.

Cont to dec 1 st at armhole edge every RS row 4 (5, 6, 7) more times, and AT THE SAME TIME, dec 1 st at neck edge every row 6 (6, 8, 8) times, then every RS row 5 (5, 4, 6) times, then every 4 rows 5 (5, 5, 4) times—13 (14, 16, 18) sts rem in left shoulder.

✱ **NOTE:** For neck edge decs, on RS rows, k2tog, work to end; on WS rows, work to last 2 sts, p2tog.

Work even until 12 (13, 14, 14) twist rows have been completed above underarm

and pieces meas the same as Left Front to shoulder shaping.

SHAPE SHOULDER USING SHORT ROWS:

On first RS row after twist row, k7 (7, 8, 9), W&T, on WS work to end.

NEXT ROW (RS): Work across all sts, picking up wrap, and working RT only on longer side of shoulder.

Work 1 more row, then place sts on holder.

BACK

Join yarn to WS of Back; work 1 row.

NEXT ROW (RS): K1, k2tog, work to last 3 sts, ssk, k1.

Dec every RS row 4 (5, 6, 7) more times, then work even until 12 (13, 14, 14) twist rows have been completed above underarm bind off.

SHAPE SHOULDERS USING SHORT ROWS:

*On next RS row, work to 6 (7, 8, 9) sts before end, W&T; repeat from * once more.

NEXT ROW (RS): Work across all sts, working RT as directed above.

Work 1 more row, working across all sts and picking up wraps—13 (14, 16, 18) sts on each end will be used to seam shoulders; the center 38 (44, 48, 52) sts will form the Back neck.

FINISHING

Turn garment inside out so RS of Front and Back are facing each other. Using 13 (14, 16, 18) sts held from Front for left shoulder and the facing sts from Back, seam shoulder using the three-needle BO. Place the 38 (44, 48, 52) center Back sts on holder and seam 2nd shoulder using rem Back sts.

NECKBAND:

With RS facing, using short circular or dpns and starting at RS, knit across held Back sts, dec 10 (11, 11, 13) sts evenly spaced; pick up and knit 45 (45, 46, 46) sts between Back neck and center Front sts; k across center Front sts, dec 5 (6, 7, 8) sts evenly spaced; pick up and knit 45 (45, 46, 46) sts between center Front and Back neck—129 (135, 144, 147) sts.

RNDS 1–4: Work Baby Cable Rib pat.

BO in twist st pat as follows:

P1, *k 2nd st on left-hand needle. Without allowing first st to fall off left-hand needle, rotate needle tips to bring tip of left-hand needle in front of right-hand needle, and use tip of left-hand needle to slip first st on right-hand needle over 2nd and off the needle—one st bound off.

Knit 1st st on left-hand needle and allow 2nd st on that needle (already knit) to drop off needle. Use tip of left-hand needle to slip 1st st on right-hand needle over 2nd and off the needle—2 sts bound off.

Purl 1 st; use tip of left-hand needle to slip 1st st on right-hand needle over 2nd and off the needle—3 sts bound off.

Rep from * until all sts are bound off.

ARMHOLE BANDS:

With RS facing, using short circular or dpns and starting at center of 10 (12, 14, 16) BO underarm sts, pick up and knit 3 (4, 4, 5) sts along 5 (6, 7, 8) bound off sts; pick up 69 (73, 76, 80) sts evenly spaced along armhole; pick up and k3 (4, 4, 5) sts along last 5 (6, 7, 8) bound off sts—75 (81, 84, 90) sts.

Work as for neckband. Repeat on 2nd armhole.

Weave in ends and block to measurements.

TWISTED-CORD BELT:

Cut three lengths of yarn, each approx 12'/3.6m long, and make a twisted cord for a belt. To wear, tie the belt comfortably under the bust, at the midpoint of the Baby Cable Band.

THIS PROJECT WAS MADE WITH 5 (5, 6, 6) skeins of Classic Elite's *Provence*, 100% mercerized cotton, 3.5oz/100g = 205yd/ 186m per skein, color #2639

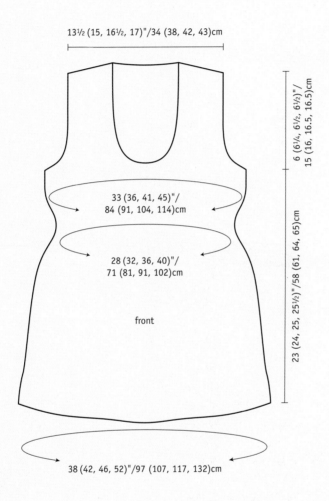

13½ (15, 16½, 17)"/34 (38, 42, 43)cm

6 (6¼, 6½, 6½)" / 15 (16, 16.5, 16.5)cm

33 (36, 41, 45)"/
84 (91, 104, 114)cm

28 (32, 36, 40)"/
71 (81, 91, 102)cm

front

23 (24, 25, 25½)"/58 (61, 64, 65)cm

38 (42, 46, 52)"/97 (107, 117, 132)cm

Feminine, beautiful—dare we say downright sexy? This piece can be worked as a top, in plain seed stitch, or as a fancy beaded evening dress. Square straps are a stylish finishing touch.

day-to-night dress

DESIGN BY **HELEN HAMANN**

EXPERIENCE LEVEL
INTERMEDIATE

SIZE S (M, L)

FINISHED MEASUREMENTS

BAND CIRCUMFERENCE: 34 (36, 38)"/86 (91, 97)cm

LENGTH, EXCLUDING STRAPS: 24 (26, 28)"/ 61 (66, 71)cm

materials

1417 (1526, 1635)yd/ 1296 (1395, 1495)m of fingering weight alpaca/silk blend yarn in black

KNITTING NEEDLES: 3.25mm (size 3 U.S.) 32"/81cm long circular needle and double pointed needles, *or size to obtain gauge for band and straps*

3.75mm (size 5 U.S.) 32"/81cm long circular needle, *or size to obtain gauge for skirt*

Stitch markers

CROCHET HOOK: size C (2.5mm)

Tapestry needle

A few yards (meters) of waste yarn and smooth, satin ribbon for provisional cast on

3 buttons, ⅜"/1cm diameter

Approx 24g black opaque 11/0 round seed beads (optional)

Beading needle (optional)

1 spool of 100% silk thread

2yd/1.8m silk lace ribbon (optional)

2yd/1.8m satin black ribbon 3"/8cm wide OR black lining fabric

gauge

26 sts and 46 rows = 4"/10cm in Seed st using smaller needles for band and straps

18 sts and 36 rows = 4"/10cm in St st using larger needles for skirt

Always take time to check your gauge.

instructions

BAND

✳ **NOTE:** Instructions are given for beaded Band. If desired, work without beads instead.

With smaller circular needles, CO 223 (235, 249) sts.

Work in St st for 23 rows ending with a RS row. Piece should meas approx 2⅛"/5cm from CO edge.

Knit next row for folding line, then work 2 more rows in St st.

With beading needle and silk thread, thread a large number of beads (about 30"/76cm long and cont threading more beads as it becomes necessary) and, holding the silk thread tog with working yarn throughout, work as foll:

NEXT ROW (RS): P1, *slip bead, p1*; rep from * to * to 1 st before end, p1 without beading. One row of Rev St st has been completed with 1 bead on each st.

NEXT ROW (WS): Purl, continuing to carry the silk thread together with the working yarn.

Work even in Seed st (with or without beads) for 20 rows.

NEXT ROW (RS): P1, *slip bead, p1*; rep from * to * to 1 st before end, p1 without beading. One row of Rev St st has been completed with 1 bead on each st.

pattern stitches

GARTER STITCH

Knit every stitch in every row.

STOCKINETTE STITCH

ROW 1 (RS): Knit.

ROW 2: Purl.

Rep rows 1 and 2 for pat.

SEED STITCH WITH BEADS

(multiple of 2 sts + 1)

ROW 1 (RS): K1, *slip bead into place and p1, k1*, rep from * to * across.

ROW 2: Purl.

Rep rows 1 and 2 for pat.

SEED STITCH WITHOUT BEADS

ROW 1 (RS): K1, p1 to end.

ROW 2: Purl.

Rep rows 1 and 2 for pat.

NEXT ROW (WS): Purl.

BO all sts. Without breaking yarn, work 1 row of Crab st (Rev sc). Cut yarn and fasten off.

SKIRT

✳ **NOTE:** The Skirt is worked in the vertical, creating a faux-pleated skirt by using short rows and a Rev St st row.

With waste yarn, ribbon, and larger circular needles, use a provisional cast on and CO 104 (114, 124) sts.

✳ **NOTE:** The colored markers are indicated here as reference only, you may have different colored markers than the ones indicated.

Place markers as foll: 4 Garter sts, pm—different color as used throughout, 20 (22, 24) sts, pm—orange, 20 (22, 24) sts, pm—green, 20 (22, 24) sts, pm—orange, 20 (22, 24) sts, pm—green.

*Change to alpaca yarn and work 2 rows in St st, working the first 4 sts of every row in Garter st throughout.

Work short row shaping as foll:

K to 1 st before last orange marker, W&T, p to end (remembering to work last 4 sts in Garter st).

K to 1 st before 1st orange marker, W&T, p to end.

K all sts working the wrap tog with wrapped st.

K next row (WS) for faux pleat.

K to 1 st before 1st green marker, W&T, p to end.

K to 1 st before last green marker, working the wrapped st tog with its wrap, W&T, p to end.

K all sts working the wrapped st tog with its wrap, p to end.

Work 2 rows in St st over all sts (except 4 garter sts).*

Rep from * to * 50(52, 54) times. Do not break yarn.

Carefully remove waste yarn from provisional CO of skirt to expose 104(114, 124) sts and place them on a spare cir needle. Cut a piece of yarn 3 times the length of the skirt and graft open sts using Kitchener st, leaving the last 10(14, 18) sts on each needle open.

BO these sts and finish with 1 row of crab st.

STRAPS (MAKE 2)

With dpn, CO 20 sts.

ROW 1 (RS): K5, pm, k11, pm, k to end.

ROW 2: P to marker, slip marker, sl1, p to marker, slip marker, sl1, p to end.

ROW 3: Knit.

Rep rows 2 and 3 until strap meas approx 18(20, 22)"/46(51, 56)cm.

Sew long selvedges of strap together to form a tube with the folding sts on both edges. BO all sts.

FINISHING

With silk thread, secure satin ribbon or lining to top and side edges of band. Fold band and with crochet hook, work 1 row of crab stitch along both sides of band. Sew silk lace ribbon (optional) to bottom front edge of band.

Pin skirt to bottom front edge of band, starting at the right edge and ending with the left edge, making sure that the skirt opening matches the band edges. With alpaca yarn threaded on a tapestry needle, use the backstitch seam to sew skirt to band in the "ditch" at the bottom edge of the band's crochet edging; the band's edging and silk lace ribbon, if used, should remain free and slightly overlap the body.

With back side facing, make 3 button loops on the right Back as follows: thread a tapestry needle with the two ends of a strand of yarn held together and secure the "loop" to the main fabric where you want the button loop to be. Bring the needle in and out of the main fabric about ¼"/6mm from the secured point and create a small loop that will accommodate the button. Bring the needle in and out at the same point where the yarn was secured. From this point on work a series of blanket stitches over the 4 strands of yarn in the loop, keeping them very close together, until the

loop has been completely covered by the blanket stitches. Secure yarn at the end. Break yarn. With silk thread on a sewing needle, secure buttons opposite button loops.

Fold band so opening is in center of Back, and Front is facing you. Lay flat on a table and carefully meas center Front and Back. Meas 4"/10cm to either side of center point and place a marker in Front and Back. From this point to the outer edge, secure strap to band grafting sts using the Kitchener method. Turn garment over so Back is facing you and pin strap's edge to the base of band where the marker has been placed 4"/10cm away from center back. Secure strap at base of band and up both sides until you reach the top edge of band. With yarn threaded on a tapestry needle, secure silk lace ribbon to outer edge of each strap (optional). Rep for other strap.

Fold in the 4 Garter sts at edge of Skirt and secure them to the WS using Running st.

Wash in cold water with mild soap or shampoo, and rinse with hair conditioner. Lay flat to dry. When slightly damp, lightly steam-block on WS.

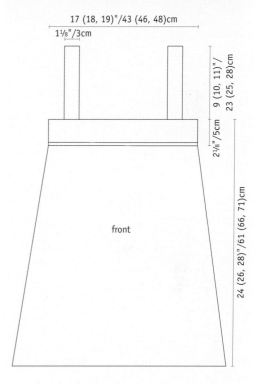

17 (18, 19)"/43 (46, 48)cm
1⅛"/3cm
9 (10, 11)"/ 23 (25, 28)cm
2⅛"/5cm
front
24 (26, 28)"/61 (66, 71)cm

THIS DRESS WAS MADE WITH 13 (14, 15) skeins of Elann.com's *Peruvian Collection Baby Silk*, 80% baby alpaca/20% silk, 1.75oz/50g = 109yd/100m per skein, color #500 Black

Replace your favorite pre-pregnancy sweatshirt with this hot hoodie. It's styled and shaped exactly like a regular sweater (just a little roomier). A two-way separating zipper lets the hoodie open at the bottom as the tummy expands.

motherhoodie

DESIGN BY **ALISON HANSEL**

EXPERIENCE LEVEL
INTERMEDIATE
SIZE S (M, L, XL)
FINISHED MEASUREMENTS
BUST: 38 (42, 46, 50)"/97 (107, 117, 127)cm
LENGTH: 23 (25½, 27, 28½)"/58 (65, 69, 72)cm

✳ **NOTE:** This length should cover that stretch panel in your maternity jeans. The pattern indicates where you can adjust length to make a more cropped version closer in length to your pre-pregnancy hoodies.

materials

1260 (1380, 1600, 1760)yd/1152 (1262, 1463, 1609)m wool or wool blend, worsted weight yarn

KNITTING NEEDLES: 5mm (size 8 U.S.) *or size to obtain gauge*

Third needle of similar size for three-needle bind off

A few yards of scrap yarn in contrasting color

Tapestry needle

2-way separating zipper bought to length after knitting is complete

Sewing needle

Sewing thread

gauge

16 sts and 24 rows = 4"/10cm over St st

Always take time to check your gauge

pattern stitch

STOCKINETTE STITCH

ROW 1 (RS): Knit.
ROW 2 (WS): Purl.

Rep rows 1 and 2 for pat.

instructions

BACK

CO 76 (84, 92, 100) sts.

Work Seed st edging as foll:

ROW 1 (WS): *K1, p1; rep from * to end.

ROW 2 (RS): *P1, k1; rep from * to end.

Repeat rows 1 and 2 twice more.

Change to St st, and beg with WS row, work 7 (7, 13, 13) rows.

DECREASES FOR WAIST SHAPING:

DEC ROW (RS): K2, ssk, k to last 4 sts, k2tog, k2—74 (82, 90, 98) sts.

Repeat dec row every 6 rows 5 more times—64 (72, 80, 88) sts.

Work 11 (17, 17, 23) rows even.

✳ **NOTE:** You can adjust the final length of the sweater by working more or fewer rows here. To keep the cardigan closer to pre-pregnancy length, try leaving out 6 rows or more of knitting. End after working a WS row.

BEGIN INCREASES:

INC ROW (RS): K2, M1L, k to last 2 sts, M1R, k2—66 (74, 82, 90) sts.

Repeat inc row every 6 rows 5 times more—76 (84, 92, 100) sts.

Work even for 5 (7, 7, 7) rows and Back meas 15 (16½, 17½, 18½)"/38 (42, 44, 47)cm or desired length to armhole.

＊ NOTE: Again, you can work more or fewer rows here, depending whether you prefer more or less belly coverage.

ARMHOLE SHAPING:

BO 4 sts at beg of next two rows—68 (76, 84, 92) sts.

Work 2 rows even.

DEC ROW (RS): K2, k2tog, k to last 4 sts, ssk, k2—66 (74, 82, 90) sts.

Repeat dec row every 4 rows 3 (4, 4, 3) more times—60 (66, 74, 84) sts.

Then rep dec row every other row 16 (17, 19, 22) times—28 (32, 36, 40) sts.

Purl one row, then BO rem 28 (32, 36, 40) sts for Back neck.

LEFT FRONT

CO 38 (42, 46, 50) sts.

Work 6 rows of Seed st edging as for Back.

NEXT ROW (WS): (K1, p1) twice, p to end.

ROW 2 (RS): K to last 4 sts, (p1, k1) twice.

Work 5 (5, 11, 11) more rows as above, maintaining 4 Edge sts in Seed st as est.

DECREASES FOR WAIST SHAPING:

DEC ROW: K2, ssk, k to last 4 sts, (p1, k1) 2 times—37 (41, 45, 49) sts.

Remembering to work 4 Edge sts in Seed st as est, rep dec row every 6 rows 5 more times—32 (36, 40, 44) sts.

Work 11 (17, 23, 23) rows even, continuing to work 4 Edge sts in Seed st as est.

✳ **NOTE:** If you adjusted the length of the Back, be sure to work the same number of rows here as on the Back.

BEGIN INCREASES:

INC ROW: K2, M1L, k to last 4 sts, (p1, k1) twice—33 (37, 41, 45) sts.

Remembering to work 4 Edge sts in Seed st as est, repeat inc row every 6 rows 5 times more—38 (42, 46, 50) sts.

Work 5 (7, 7, 7) rows even, cont to work 4 Edge sts in Seed st as est, or until Front matches Back to armhole. End after completing a WS row.

ARMHOLE SHAPING:

NEXT ROW (RS): BO 4 sts at beg of row—34 (38, 42, 46) sts.

Work 3 rows even, cont to work 4 Edge sts in Seed st as est.

DEC ROW (RS): K2, k2tog, k to last 4 sts, (p1, k1) 2 times. 33 (37, 41, 45) sts.

Rep dec row every 4 rows 3 (4, 4, 3) more times, continuing to work 4 Edge sts in Seed st as est—30 (33, 37, 42) sts.

Then rep dec row every other row 6 (7, 9, 12) times, continuing to work 4 Edge sts in Seed st as est—24 (26, 28, 30) sts.

NECK SHAPING:

ROW 1 (WS): BO 4 (4, 6, 6) sts, p to end—20 (22, 22, 24) sts.

ROW 2 (AND ALL RS ROWS): K2, k2tog, k to end.

ROW 3: BO 2 (4, 4, 4) sts, p to end—17 (17, 17, 19) sts.

ROW 5: BO 2 (2, 2, 3) sts, p to end—14 (14, 14, 15) sts.

ROW 7: BO 1 (1, 1, 2) st, p to end—12 (12, 12, 12) sts.

ROW 9: BO 1 (1, 1, 1) st, p to end. 10 (10, 10, 10) sts.

With neck shaping complete, continue to work armhole dec (as in Row 2) on next and every RS row a total of 6 more times—4 sts rem.

Purl 1 row, then BO.

RIGHT FRONT

CO 38 (42, 46, 50) sts.

Work 6 rows of Seed st edging as for Back.

NEXT ROW (WS): P to last 4 sts, (k1, p1) twice.

ROW 2 (RS): (P1, k1) twice, k to end.

Work 5 (5, 11, 11) more rows

as above, maintaining 4 Edge sts in Seed st as est.

DECREASES FOR WAIST SHAPING:

DEC ROW: (P1, k1) twice, k to last 4 sts, k2tog, k2—37 (41, 45, 49) sts.

Remembering to work 4 Edge sts in Seed st as est, repeat dec row every 6 rows 5 more times—32 (36, 40, 44) sts.

Work 11 (17, 23, 23) rows even, continuing to work 4 Edge sts in Seed st as est.

✳ **NOTE:** If you adjusted the length of the Back, be sure to work same number of rows here as on Back.

INCREASES:

INC ROW: (P1, k1) twice, k to last 2 sts, m1right, k2—33 (37, 41, 45) sts.

Remembering to work 4 Edge sts in Seed st as est, rep inc row every 6 rows 5 more times—38 (42, 46, 50) sts.

Work even for 6 (8, 8, 8) rows, continuing to work 4 Edge sts in Seed st as est, or until Front matches Back to armhole. End after completing a RS row.

ARMHOLE SHAPING:

NEXT ROW (WS): BO 4 sts at beg of row—34 (38, 42, 46) sts.

Work 2 rows even, cont to work 4 Edge sts in Seed st as est.

DEC ROW: (P1, k1) twice, k to last 4 sts, ssk, k2—33 (37, 41, 45) sts.

Repeat dec row every 4 rows 3 (4, 4, 3) more times, continuing to work 4 Edge sts in Seed st as est—30 (33, 37, 42) sts.

Then rep dec row every other row 6 (7, 9, 12) times, continuing to work 4 Edge sts in Seed st as est—24 (26, 28, 30) sts.

Work 1 WS row.

NECK SHAPING:

ROW 1 (RS): BO 4 (4, 6, 6) sts, k to last 4 sts, ssk, k2—19 (21, 21, 23) sts.

ROW 2 (AND ALL WS ROWS): P to end.

ROW 3: BO 2 (4, 4, 4) sts, k to last 4 sts, ssk, k2—16 (16, 16, 18) sts.

ROW 5: BO 2 (2, 2, 3) sts, k to last 4 sts, ssk, k2—13 (13, 13, 14) sts.

ROW 7: BO 1 (1, 1, 2) st, k to last 4 sts, ssk, k2—11 (11, 11, 11) sts.

BO 1 (1, 1, 1) st, k to last 4 sts, ssk, k2—9 (9, 9, 9) sts.

With neck shaping complete, cont to work armhole dec at armhole edge every RS row 5 more times—4 sts rem.

Purl one row, then BO.

SLEEVES (MAKE 2)

With long tail cast on, CO 36 (38, 40, 42) sts. Work 6 rows of Seed st edging as for Back. Switch to St st, and beg with a WS row, work 9 rows.

SLEEVE SHAPING:

INC ROW: K2, M1L, k to last 4, M1R, k2—38 (40, 42, 44) sts.

Rep inc row every 8 rows 7 (8, 9, 10) more times— 52 (56, 60, 64) sts.

Work even until Sleeve meas 18 (19, 19 1/2, 20)"/46 (48, 50, 51)cm or desired length to beg of sleeve cap. End after completing a WS row.

CAP SHAPING:

BO 4 sts at beg of next 2 rows—44 (48, 52, 56) sts.

Work 2 rows even.

DEC ROW: K2, k2tog, k to last 4 sts, ssk, k2—42 (46, 50, 54) sts.

Repeat dec row every 4 rows 3 (4, 4, 3) times more— 36 (38, 42, 48) sts.

Then rep dec row every other row 15 (16, 18, 21) times— 6 sts.

Purl 1 row.

NEXT ROW: K2, k2tog, k2— 5 sts.

Purl one row, then BO.

FINISHING

Block all pieces, paying particular attention to Front center Seed st edges, which need to lay flat to sew in zipper.

HOOD:

Using Mattress st, sew Sleeves into armholes. With RS facing and beg at beg of right neck, pick up 18 (20, 22, 24) sts along right neck edge, 3 sts from right Sleeve, 30 sts from Back, 3 sts from left Sleeve, and 18 (20, 22, 24) sts down left neck—72 (76, 80, 84) sts.

ROW 1 (WS): Work 4 sts in Seed st (maintaining pat), p to last 4 sts, work 4 sts in Seed st (maintaining pat).

ROW 2 (RS): Work 4 sts in Seed st, k to last 4 sts, work 4 sts in Seed st.

Rep rows 1 and 2 until Hood meas 15 (15, 16, 16)"/38 (38, 43, 43)cm.

Divide sts over two needles. Fold Hood in half so that WS is facing out and needles are parallel to each other. With third needle, work three-needle bind off to close top of Hood.

RIGHT FRONT POCKET:

Count 12 (12, 18, 18) rows up from top of bottom Seed st edging on right Front. With scrap yarn, baste line across that row from center Seed st edging to outer edge. Beg after last stitch of center Seed st edging, pick up 25 (27, 29, 31) sts along the row above basting line, ending 7 (9, 11, 13) sts from outer edge.

ROW 1 (WS): (K1, p1) twice, p to end.

ROW 2 (RS): K to last 4 sts, (p1, k1) twice.

Continuing to work 4 Edge sts in Seed st as est above, work 3 more rows.

DEC ROW: K to last 6 sts, k2tog, (p1, k1) twice—24 (26, 28, 30) sts.

Rep dec row every 6 rows 3 more times, continuing to work Seed st edge as est—21 (23, 25, 27) sts.

Work one WS row, then BO all sts. Graft top of pocket to front panel along the row just above the final decrease row of front waist shaping. Sew side of pocket to center Seed st edging using Mattress st.

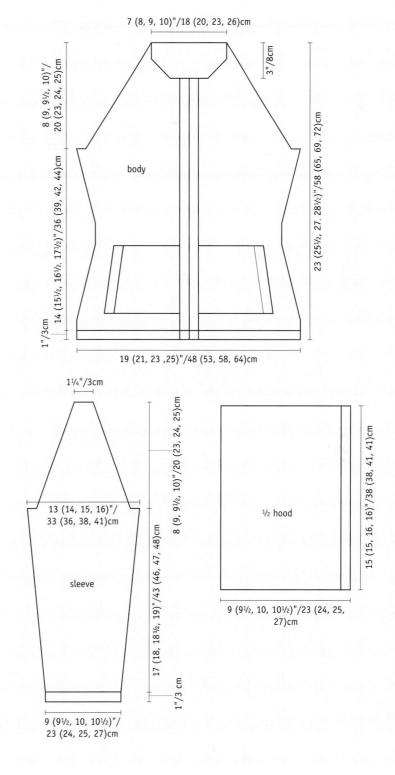

7 (8, 9, 10)"/18 (20, 23, 26)cm

3"/8cm

8 (9, 9½, 10)"/ 20 (23, 24, 25)cm

body

23 (25½, 27, 28½)"/58 (65, 69, 72)cm

14 (15½, 16½, 17½)"/36 (39, 42, 44)cm

1"/3cm

19 (21, 23 ,25)"/48 (53, 58, 64)cm

1¼"/3cm

13 (14, 15, 16)"/ 33 (36, 38, 41)cm

sleeve

8 (9, 9½, 10)"/20 (23, 24, 25)cm

17 (18, 18½, 19)"/43 (46, 47, 48)cm

1"/3 cm

9 (9½, 10, 10½)"/ 23 (24, 25, 27)cm

½ hood

15 (15, 16, 16)"/38 (38, 41, 41)cm

9 (9½, 10, 10½)"/23 (24, 25, 27)cm

LEFT FRONT POCKET:

Count 12 (12, 18, 18) rows up from top of bottom Seed st edging on left Front. With scrap yarn, baste line across that row from outer edge to beginning of center Seed st edging. Beginning 7 (9, 11, 13) sts from outer edge, pick up 25 (27, 29, 31) sts along row above basting line, ending with last st before center Seed st edge.

ROW 1 (WS): P to last 4 sts, (k1, p1) twice.

ROW 2 (RS): (P1, k1) twice, k to end.

Continuing to work 4 Edge sts in Seed st as est above, work 3 more rows.

DEC ROW: (P1, k1) 2 times, ssk, k to end—24 (26, 28, 30) sts.

Rep dec row every 6 rows 3 more times, continuing to work Seed st edge as est—21 (23, 25, 27) sts.

Work one WS row, then BO all sts. Graft top of pocket to front panel along the row just above the final decrease row of front waist shaping. Sew side of pocket to center Seed st edging using Mattress st.

Sew side and Sleeve seams with Mattress st. Weave in all remaining ends. Purchase a two-way separating zipper to match the length of the front opening on your finished sweater. Pin and sew zipper into place, making sure to line up pockets and top of neck.

THIS PROJECT WAS MADE WITH 12 (13, 15, 17) balls of Noro's *Silk Garden*, 45% silk/45% kid mohair/10% lambswool, 1.75oz/50g = 110yd/100m per ball, color #211

This fresh and flirty design can accommodate a growing belly all the way to the third trimester. The bodice has two elastic bands for added support, and the longer length in front provides ample coverage. Wear it alone as a mini-dress, over skinny jeans, or as a swimsuit cover-up.

a-symm tube top

DESIGN BY **ASHLEY MONCRIEF**

EXPERIENCE LEVEL
INTERMEDIATE

SIZE S (M, L, XL)

FINISHED MEASUREMENTS
(unstretched)

BUST: 32 (35, 39, 43)"/
81 (89, 99, 109)cm

LENGTH (SHORT SIDE):
22½ (23, 24, 25)"/57 (58, 61, 64)cm

✻ **NOTE:** Front is 1½"/4cm longer than back.

materials

1100 (1225, 1430, 1640)yd/1006 (1120, 1308, 1500)m of soy or soy blend worsted weight yarn in multi-colors

KNITTING NEEDLES:
5.75mm (size 10 U.S.) circular needle 24"/61cm long *or size needed to obtain gauge*

5mm (size 8 U.S.) circular needle 32"/81cm long

1yd/.9m each of 1¼"/3.2cm-wide and ¾"/1.9cm-wide elastic

Stitch markers of different colors

gauge

21 sts and 28 rnds = 4"/10cm over Texture st

Always take time to check your gauge.

pattern stitches

TEXTURE STITCH (CIRCULAR)

RND 1 (AND ALL ODD RNDS): Knit.

RND 2: K1, *insert RH needle from behind under running thread between st just worked and next st, thus putting an extra strand on the needle, k next 2 sts, then with LH needle pass extra strand over 2 k sts, k2; rep from *, end k1.

RND 4: K3, rep from * of rnd 2, end last rep k1.

Rep rnds 1–4 for pat.

TEXTURE STITCH (BACK AND FORTH)

RND 1 (AND ALL WS RNDS): Purl.

ROWS 2 AND 4: Work as for circular pat.

Rep rows 1–4 for pat.

THIS PROJECT WAS MADE WITH 7 (8, 9, 10) balls of South West Trading Company's *Phoenix*, 100% soy silk, 3.5oz/100g = 175yd/ 160m per ball, color # 506 Canyon

instructions

✳ **NOTE:** To incorporate short row shaping into the pattern stitch, work the first leg of the short row as usual. After you turn the work, purl back to the point where you turn the work again. Then, on the final leg of the short row shaping, remember to use the row from the pattern stitch that you didn't use on the first leg (work row 2 if you started with row 4, and vice versa). To finish the round after the halfway marker, continue on as though completing the first leg of the short row (if you started with row 2 of pattern stitch, switch back to row 2 for remainder of round). Incorporate increases and decreases into the pattern st at the two side "seams" of the garment. Work extra sts in St st until you have an even number to incorporate them.

BODY

Using larger needles, CO 24 (32, 46, 62) sts.

Beg working in Texture st.

Starting with 2nd row, inc 4 sts at each end of every WS row as foll: CO 2 sts, p1, m1, p1, m1, p to 2 sts before end, m1, p1, m1, p1, CO 2 sts.

Once you have 224 (232, 246, 262) sts on the needles, join and beg working in the round. Place marker to denote beg of rnd, work 112 (116, 123, 131) sts, place halfway point marker, work 112 (116, 123, 131) sts to end of rnd.

Work 14 rnds even in pat as est.

SHORT ROW SHAPING

(RND 15): Work to 2 sts before halfway marker, W&T, p back to 2 sts before beg, W&T, work to end.

Rep short row shaping every 8 rnds 6 times more. AT THE SAME TIME, beg dec as foll:

SIZES M, L, AND XL ONLY (RND 16, DEC RND): *K1, k2tog, work to 3 sts before halfway marker, ssk, k1, slip halfway marker, k1, k2tog, work to 3 sts before end, ssk, k1—4 sts decreased. Work 5 rnds even; rep from * 3 (8, 12) more times.

ALL SIZES (RND 16 FOR SIZE S): *Work dec rnd as above, work 3 rnds even; rep from * 14 (11, 5, 0) more times. Work 1 rnd even.

SIZE S ONLY: *Dec rnd, work 1 rnd even; rep from * 3 times— 148 (168, 186, 206) sts on the needles.

NEXT RND: Inc 18 (18, 20, 22) sts evenly around—166 (186, 206, 226) sts.

Work 16 (10, 10, 10) rnds even; *dec rnd, work 5 rnds even; rep from * 2 (3, 3, 3) more times—154 (170, 190, 210) sts rem.

BO all sts.

RUFFLE TRIM:

Using smaller needles, pick up 155 (170, 190, 210) sts evenly around top edge of garment.

RND 1: *P3, m1, k2, m1; rep from * to end.

RND 2: *P3, k4; rep from * to end.

RND 3: *P3, m1, k4, m1; rep from * to end.

RND 4: *P3, k6; rep from * to end.

RND 5: *P3, m1, k6, m1; rep from * to end.

RND 6: *P3, k8; rep from * to end.

BO all sts. Weave in ends.

Block the garment to specified measurements.

ELASTIC BANDS:

Cut wider band to 24 (27, 31, 35)"/61 (69, 79, 89)cm. Sew ends tog and pin to inside of garment at the most narrow point, right below where the inc were made for the bust. Attach elastic to the garment using the Herringbone st (see page 123).

Cut narrower band to 25 (28, 32, 36)"/64 (71, 81, 91)cm. Sew ends tog and pin to inside of garment at the top hem just below where the ruffle begins. Attach elastic to the garment using the Herringbone st.

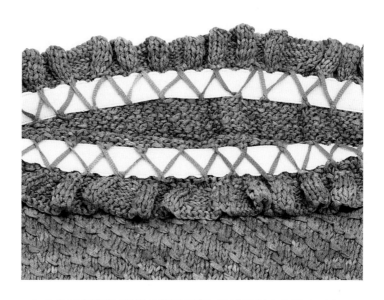

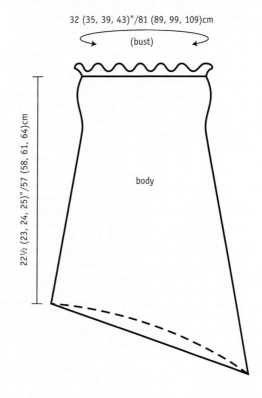

32 (35, 39, 43)"/81 (89, 99, 109)cm

(bust)

22½ (23, 24, 25)"/57 (58, 61, 64)cm

body

Softly green, gently bumpy... sounds like a delectable snack! The unusual Puckered-Stitch pattern is perfect for maternity wear, because it hides a multitude of little bulges while still clinging to feminine curves. More experienced knitters will find the fabulous cutout shape an unusual knitting challenge.

the gherkin tunic

DESIGN BY **ASHLEY MONCRIEF**

EXPERIENCE LEVEL

INTERMEDIATE

SIZE S (M, L, XL)

FINISHED MEASUREMENTS
(unstretched)

BUST: 32 (35, 39, 43)"/81 (89, 99, 109)cm

HIP: 38 (40, 42, 45)"/97 (102, 107, 114)cm

LENGTH IN BACK: 29½ (30, 31, 31½)"/75 (76, 79, 80)cm

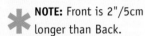 **NOTE:** Front is 2"/5cm longer than Back.

materials

1560 (1660, 1795, 1950)yd/1426 (1518, 1641, 1783)m of mohair or mohair blend DK weight yarn

KNITTING NEEDLES: 3.25mm (size 5 U.S.) circular needle 24"/61cm long *or size to obtain gauge*

Stitch markers of different colors

gauge

25 sts and 40 rnds = 4"/10cm in pattern stitch

Always take time to check your gauge.

pattern stitches

PUCKER STITCH

To make pucker, pick up the running thread 12 rounds beneath the next stitch and put on the left-hand needle; knit that thread together with the next stitch (this forms a pucker in the fabric).

RNDS 1–11: Knit.

RND 12: K12, *Make pucker, k4, make pucker, k18. Rep from * around.

RNDS 13–23: Knit.

RND 24: *Make pucker, k4, make pucker, k18. Rep from * around.

Rep rnds 1–24 for pat.

GARTER STITCH

RND 1: Knit.

RND 2: Purl.

Rep rnds 1 and 2 for pat.

instructions

✳ **NOTE:** Do not work short row shaping on rnds 12 or 24 of the pattern stitch (the rounds where the puckers are made). When incorporating decreases and increases into the pattern stitch, either subtract or add the stitches first from the 18 knit stitches and not from the segment of "make pucker, k4, make pucker." When those 18 stitches are gone (in decreases), take the decreases out of the "make pucker, k4, make pucker" segment at the side "seams." This means that some of the puckers on the sides of the garment will be closer together than in the rest of the pattern. This variance will be unnoticeable in the finished garment.

CO 250 (264, 276, 294) sts, pm after 125 (132, 138, 147) sts to mark halfway point and a second marker of a different color to mark beg of rnd.

Work 8 rnds even in Garter st.

Change to Pucker st.

When garment reaches 1"/2.5cm long, beg short row shaping: *k to 1 st before halfway marker, W&T, work in St st back to 1 st before beg of rnd, W&T, complete rnd (when you come to the yarn wraps where you turned your work, k into the wrap and the next st

tog to hide the wraps).

Rep short row shaping every 1"/2.5cm for the next 10"/25cm.

AT THE SAME TIME, when front of garment reaches 5½ (6, 7, 7½)"/14 (15, 18, 19)cm long, work dec rnd as foll: *k1, k2tog, k to 3 sts before halfway marker, ssk, slip marker, k1, k2tog, k to 3 sts before end of rnd, ssk, k1 (4 sts dec).

Rep dec rnd every 1"/2.5cm for the next 12 (10, 7, 5)"/ 31 (25, 18, 13)cm—52 (44, 32, 24) sts dec. Work even until front of garment meas 24½ (25, 26, 26½)"/62 (64, 66, 67)cm.

SLEEVES

K1 rnd even until 5 sts before the end of rnd. BO next 10 sts, CO 65 (65, 69, 69) sts and k these new sts. K to 5 sts before halfway marker, BO next 10 sts, CO 65 (65, 69, 69) sts, and k these new sts. Work to end.

K4 rnds even. For the first 4 rnds of the Sleeves work the Sleeves only (each set of newly cast-on sts) in Garter st.

DIAGONAL SLASH OPENING:

K55 (61, 67, 73), BO 10, k to end of rnd. Work to 1 st before BO sts, k2tog, turn work. BO 9, work in St st (purling) all the way around, past beg of rnd and halfway marker, back to BO sts. Turn work. *K back

around to 1 st before BO sts. K2tog, turn, BO 9 (9, 11, 11) sts, work back around to BO sts. CO 10 sts, turn. Rep from * 1 time.

K back around to 1 st before BO sts, k2tog, turn, BO 3 sts, work back around to BO sts. CO 10 sts, turn. *K back around to BO sts, turn, work back around to BO sts, CO 10 (10, 12, 12) sts, turn. Rep from * once more. K back around to BO sts, turn, work back around to BO sts, CO 4 sts, turn. K back around to BO sts, and close the opening by joining work and k across all sts evenly to the end of rnd.

AT THE SAME TIME (as diagonal slash opening) and starting just after the first 4 rnds of the Sleeves, work dec rnd as foll: dec 32 (35, 39, 41) sts evenly across (outside of the diagonal slash opening) using k2tog.

Rep dec rnd every 1"/2.5cm for the next 6"/15cm. On next rnd, *k1, k2tog. rep from * to end of rnd. Work 4 rnds more, then BO loosely.

THIS PROJECT WAS MADE WITH 11 (12, 13, 14) balls of GGH Yarns' *Soft-Kid*, 70% super kid mohair/25% nylon/5% wool, .9oz/25g = 151yd/138m per ball, color #54 Moss.

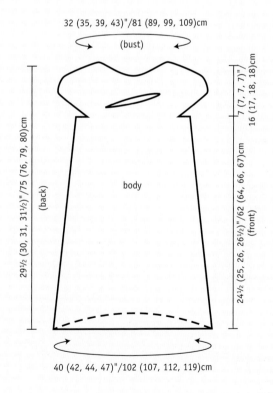

32 (35, 39, 43)"/81 (89, 99, 109)cm

(bust)

7 (7, 7, 7)"
16 (17, 18, 18)cm

29½ (30, 31, 31½)"/75 (76, 79, 80)cm

(back)

body

24½ (25, 26, 26½)"/62 (64, 66, 67)cm
(front)

40 (42, 44, 47)"/102 (107, 112, 119)cm

This sleeveless tank features an elegant lace panel on both the front and back. Knit in worsted weight cotton and viscose yarn, it's cool, comfortable, and quicker to knit than most lace designs.

lacy vine tank

DESIGN BY **ELIZABETA NEDELJKOVICH-MARTONOSI**

instructions

BACK

Using smaller needles, CO 82 (90, 100, 110) sts.

Set up Lacy Vines pat:

ROW 1 (RS): K20 (24, 29, 34) sts, pm, work 5 rep of Lacy Vines pat over next 42 sts, pm, k20 (24, 29, 34) sts.

ROW 2: P20 (24, 29, 34) sts, slip marker, work 5 rep of Lacy Vines pat, p20 (24, 29, 34) sts.

Work another 4 rows in pat as est, with St st on sides and Lacy Vines pat in the center. Change to larger needles and cont in pats as est until piece meas 14½ (15¼, 16, 17)"/37 (39, 41, 43)cm from CO edge. End after completing a WS row.

ARMHOLE SHAPING:

BO 3 (4, 4, 5) sts at beg of next 2 rows, then BO 3 sts at beg of next 2 rows.

BO 2 sts at beg of next 2 rows, then dec 1 st at beg of next

4 rows—60 (68, 78, 86) sts rem.

Work even in pats as est until armhole meas 6 (6½, 7, 7½)"/15 (17, 18, 19)cm. End after completing a WS row.

NECK SHAPING:

NEXT ROW (RS): Work 16 (18, 21, 23) sts in pat, BO center 28 (32, 36, 40) sts, work to end of row.

NEXT ROW (WS): Work even in pats as est.

NEXT ROW: BO 2 sts, work to end of row.

NEXT ROW: Dec 1 st at end of row.

BO rem 13 (15, 18, 20) sts. Cut yarn. With WS facing, attach yarn to left shoulder at neck edge. BO 2 sts, work to end of row.

NEXT ROW: Dec 1 st at end of row.

Work even until armhole measures 7 (7½, 8, 8½)"/18 (19, 20, 22)cm.

BO rem 13 (15, 18, 20) sts.

EXPERIENCE LEVEL

INTERMEDIATE

SIZE S (M, L, XL)

FINISHED MEASUREMENTS

BUST: 33 (36, 40, 44)"/83 (90, 102, 112)cm

LENGTH: 21½ (19¼, 20½, 22)"/55 (50, 52, 55.5)cm

materials

704 (704, 880, 880)yd/644 (644, 805, 805)m cotton/viscose blend worsted weight yarn in brown

KNITTING NEEDLES: 4mm (size 6 U.S.) *or size to obtain gauge*

3mm (size 4 U.S.)

Tapestry needle

gauge

20 sts and 24 rows = 4"/10cm over St st using larger needles

Always take time to check your gauge.

pattern stitch

LACY VINES PATT

Multiple of 8 sts + 2

ROW 1: *P2, k6, *p2.

ROW 2 (AND ALL EVEN ROWS): *K2, p6; rep from * to last 2 sts, *k2.

ROW 3: *P2, yo, k2, sl 1, k1, psso, k2; rep from * to last 2 sts, *p2.

ROW 5: *P2, k1, yo, k2, sl 1, k1, psso, k1; rep from * to last 2 sts, *p2.

ROW 7: *P2, k2, yo, k2, sl 1, k1, psso; rep from * to last 2 sts, *p2.

ROW 9: *P2, k6; rep from * to last 2 sts, *p2.

ROW 11: *P2, k2, k2tog, k2, yo; rep from * to last 2 sts, *p2.

ROW 13: *P2, k1, k2tog, k2, yo, k1; rep from * to last 2 sts, *p2.

ROW 15: *P2, k2tog, k2, yo, k2; rep from * to last 2 sts, *p2.

Repeat rows 1–16 for patt.

FRONT

Work as for the Back until armhole meas 3½ (4½, 4½, 5)"/9 (11, 11, 13)cm. End after completing a WS row.

NECK SHAPING:

BO the center 20 (24, 28, 32) sts.

Working both shoulders AT THE SAME TIME using 2 separate balls of yarn, BO 3 sts at neck edge once, then BO 2 sts at neck edge once, then BO 1 st at neck edge twice.

Work even until neck opening meas 3½"/9cm and matches back length, BO rem 13 (15, 18, 20) sts on each shoulder.

FINISHING

Sew one shoulder seam.

NECKBAND:

With smaller needles and RS facing, pick up 140 (130, 148, 150) sts evenly around the neck opening. Work 5 rows in St st, beg with a WS row. BO. Sew the other shoulder seam, including the neckband seam.

ARMHOLE BANDS:

With smaller needles and RS facing, pick up 80 (74, 86, 92) sts evenly around armhole opening. Work 5 rows in St st, beg with a WS row. BO. Rep on 2nd armhole. Sew side seams, including the armhole band seam.

THIS PROJECT WAS KNIT WITH custom yarn created by the designer, made from 3 strands of cotton, 3 strands of viscose (rayon), and 1 strand of straw rayon held together.

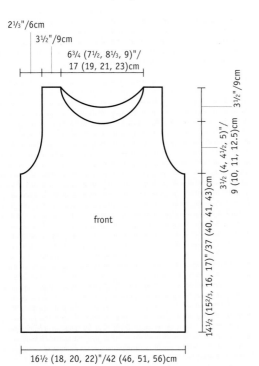

2⅓"/6cm

3½"/9cm

6¾ (7½, 8⅓, 9)"/ 17 (19, 21, 23)cm

front

3½"/9cm

3½ (4, 4½, 5)"/ 9 (10, 11, 12.5)cm

14½ (15⅔, 16, 17)"/37 (40, 41, 43)cm

16½ (18, 20, 22)"/42 (46, 51, 56)cm

Steal a little style with this Chanel-style jacket—perfect for the office or a night on the town. The slip-stitch color pattern looks challenging, but it is actually quite easy, because you only use one color in each row.

houndstooth check jacket

DESIGN BY **ELIZABETA NEDELJKOVICH-MARTONOSI**

EXPERIENCE LEVEL

INTERMEDIATE

SIZE S (M, L, XL)

FINISHED MEASUREMENTS

BUST: 35 (38, 41, 44)"/ 89 (97, 104, 112)cm

LENGTH: 16½ (17½, 17¾, 19)"/42 (44, 45, 48.5)cm

materials

APPROX TOTAL: 800 (800, 1200, 1200)yd/732 (732, 1097, 1097)m Aran weight cotton/acrylic blend yarn:

COLOR A: 400 (400, 600, 600)yd/366 (366, 549, 549)m in beige

COLOR B: 400 (400, 600, 600)yd/366 (366, 549, 549)m in black

KNITTING NEEDLES: 5mm (size 8 U.S.), *or size to obtain gauge*

3.5mm (size 4 U.S.)

3.5mm (size 4 U.S.) circular needle 24"/61cm long

1 large button, approx 1"/2.5cm diameter

Sewing needle and thread to match button

Tapestry needle

gauge

18 sts and 26 rows = 4"/10cm using larger needles

Always take time to check your gauge.

pattern stitch

FLECKED TWEED STITCH

Worked over a multiple of 4 sts + 3.

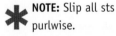 **NOTE:** Slip all sts purlwise.

ROW 1 (WS): Using A, p1, yb, sl 1, yf, *p3, yb, sl 1, yf, rep from * to last st, p1.

ROW 2: Using A, k1, sl 1, *k3, sl 1; rep from * to last st, k1.

ROW 3: Using B, p3, *yb, sl 1, yf, p3, rep from * to end.

ROW 4: Using B, k3, *sl 1, k3: rep from * to end.

Repeat rows 1–4 for pat.

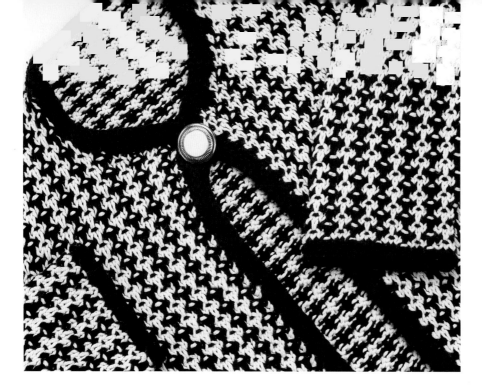

THIS PROJECT WAS MADE WITH Aunt Lydia's *Denim Quick Crochet*, 75% cotton/25% acrylic, 400yd/365m per ball:

(A) 1 (1, 2, 2) balls, color Black

(B) 1 (1, 2, 2) balls, color Beige

instructions

BACK

With color B and smaller needles, CO 79 (87, 91, 99) sts.

Knit 5 rows.

NEXT ROW (WS): Change to larger needles, add color A, and beg working Flecked Tweed st.

Work even in pat until piece meas 9 (9½, 9½, 10)"/23 (24, 24, 25)cm from CO edge. End after completing a WS row.

ARMHOLE SHAPING:

BO 3 (4, 4, 5) sts at beg of next 2 rows, then BO 3 sts at beg of next 2 rows, then BO 2 sts at beg of next 2 rows, then dec 1 st at beg of next 2 rows—61 (67, 71, 77) sts rem.

Work even until armhole meas 7½ (8, 8¼, 9)"/19 (20, 21, 23)cm.

BO all sts.

LEFT FRONT

With color B and smaller needles, CO 39 (43, 47, 51) sts.

Knit 5 rows.

NEXT ROW (WS): Change to larger needles, add color A, and beg working Flecked Tweed st.

Work even in pat until piece meas 9 (9½, 9½, 10)"/23 (24, 24, 25)cm from CO edge. End after working a WS row.

ARMHOLE SHAPING:

NEXT ROW (RS): BO 3 (4, 4, 5) sts at beg of row.

BO 3 sts at beg of next RS row, then BO 2 sts at beg of next RS row, then dec 1 st at beg of next RS row—30 (33, 37, 40) sts rem.

Work even until armhole meas 3½ (4, 4¼, 5)"/9 (10, 11, 13)cm. End after completing RS row.

NECK SHAPING:

NEXT ROW (WS): BO 4 (5, 5, 6) sts at beg of row.

BO 3 sts at beg of next WS row, then BO 2 sts at beg of next WS row, then dec 1 st at beg of next WS row—20 (22, 26, 28) sts rem.

Work even until piece meas same as back at shoulder. BO all sts.

RIGHT FRONT

Work as for Left Front to armhole shaping. End after completing a RS row.

ARMHOLE SHAPING:

NEXT ROW (WS): BO 3 (4, 4, 5) sts at beg of row.

BO 3 sts at beg of next WS row, then BO 2 sts at beg of next WS row, then dec 1 st at beg of next WS row—30 (33, 37, 40) sts rem.

Work even until armhole meas 3½ (4, 4¼, 5)"/9 (10, 11, 13) cm. End after completing a WS row.

NECK SHAPING:

NEXT ROW (RS): BO 4 (5, 5, 6) sts at beg of row.

BO 3 sts at beg of next RS row, then BO 2 sts at beg of next RS row, then dec 1 st at beg of next RS row—20 (22, 26, 28) sts rem.

Work even until piece meas same as back at shoulder. BO.

SLEEVES (MAKE 2)

With smaller needles and color B, CO 43 (47, 47, 51) sts.

Knit 5 rows.

NEXT ROW (WS): Change to larger needles, add color A, and beg working Flecked Tweed st.

Work another 6 rows in pats as est.

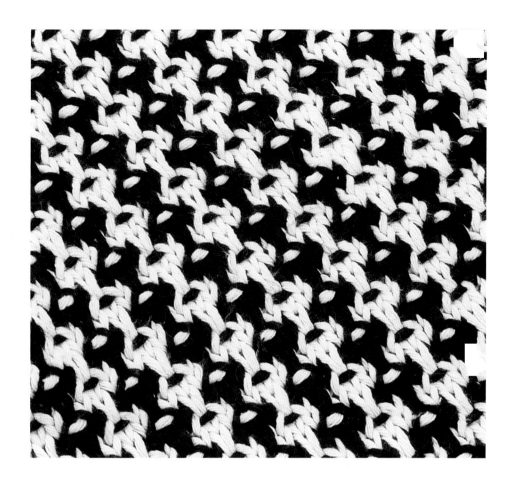

SLEEVE SHAPING:

Inc 1 st at each end of next row and then every 6 rows 8 (9, 9, 10) more times—61 (67, 67, 73) sts.

Work even until Sleeve meas 11½ (12½, 12½, 13½)"/ 29 (32, 32, 34)cm. End after completing a WS row.

CAP SHAPING:

BO 3 (4, 4, 5) st at beg of next 2 rows, then BO 3 sts at beg of next 2 rows, then BO 2 sts at beg of next 2 rows, then

dec 1 st at each end of every other row 11 (12, 12, 13) times.

BO 2 sts at beg of next 2 rows, then BO 3 sts at beg of next 2 rows.

BO rem 13 (15, 15, 17) sts.

FINISHING

Block pieces to measurements. Sew shoulder seams. Set in Sleeves, sew side and Sleeve seams.

With circular needle and color

B, evenly pick up 118 (126, 126, 134) sts along front edges and around neck.

Knit 2 rows.

ROW 3: Knit to the RS of the collar, BO 2 sts for buttonhole.

ROW 4: Knit, casting on 2 sts over buttonhole.

Knit 1 more row. BO.

Sew the button on to the Left Front to correspond with the buttonhole.

Weave in ends.

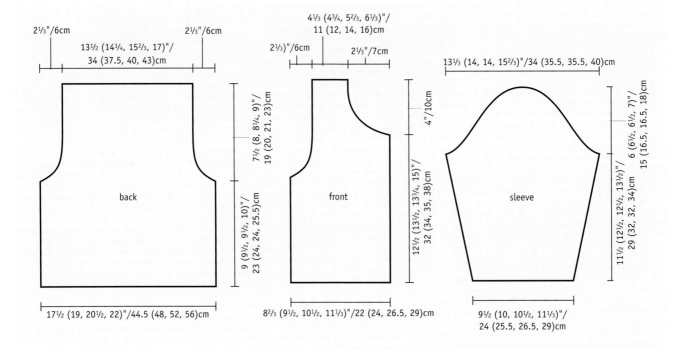

This close-fitting, lightweight sleeveless top is versatile and a little bit daring. With side laces and contrasting side panels, it can be laced as tightly or as loosely as needed. Take out the panels when the extra space is no longer needed.

abigail hemp top

DESIGN BY **CHERYL NIAMATH**

EXPERIENCE LEVEL

INTERMEDIATE

SIZE S (M, L, XL)

FINISHED MEASUREMENTS

BUST: 32 (35, 39, 43)"/81 (89, 99,109)cm, unstretched

Finished garment should fit closely at the bust line. Inserting panels will add 9 (10, 12, 12)"/20 (23, 28, 28)cm at the hips, decreasing gradually to ½"/1.3cm just below the bust.

LENGTH: 22½ (24½, 27, 27)"/57 (62, 69, 69)cm

materials

Approx total: 665 (740, 820, 885)yd/608 (677, 750, 809)m fingering weight hemp or hemp blend yarn:

Color A: 585 (650, 720, 785)yd/ 535 (594, 658, 718)m in black

Color B: 80 (90, 100,100)yd/ 73 (82, 91, 91)m in tan

KNITTING NEEDLES: 3.75mm (size 5 U.S.) *or size needed to obtain gauge*

A few yards (m) of smooth, worsted weight yarn in a contrasting color for provisional cast on

9yd/8m of ¹⁄₁₆"/1.6mm satin ribbon, cut into 4 equal lengths

CROCHET HOOKS: 4mm (size G-6 U.S.) and 2.75mm (size C-2 U.S.)

Tapestry needle

Stitch markers

gauge

24 st and 30 rows = 4"/10cm over St st, after blocking

Always take time to check your gauge.

✳ **NOTE:** Knitted fabric will be very open and stretchy.

pattern stitches

EYELET EDGE STITCH

ROWS 1–5: K4, work to last 4 st, k4.

ROW 6: K2, yo, k2tog, work to last 4 st, k2tog, yo, k2.

Rep rows 1–6 for pat.

✳ **NOTE:** Every time you make a yo, take a second to check that the right and left sides are matching. When you are working the Front, check every once in a while that the front edge stitches are lining up with the back ones. It is important that the eyelets are in line with each other.

ARMHOLE EDGE STITCH

RS ROWS: K1, p1, k1 work to last 3 sts, k1, p1, k1.

WS ROWS: P1, k1, p1, work to last 3 sts, p1, k1, p1.

special stitch used

DOUBLE LIFTED INCREASE (DLI)

Insert right-hand needle into the front of right "shoulder" of the next st in the row below and knit; then knit the st on needle; finally, insert right-hand needle into the front of left "shoulder" of the same st in the row below.

instructions

✳ **NOTE:** Work all shaping increases and decreases between edge stitches (i.e., after working the edge stitch at the right side of your piece, and before working the edge stitch at the left side of your piece).

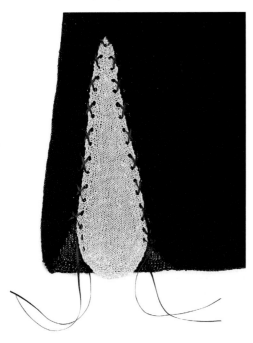

BACK

Using a provisional cast on, CO 98 (110, 120, 132) sts.

ROW 1 (RS): Knit.

ROW 2: K4, p to last 4 st, k4.

ROW 3: K2, yo, k2tog, k to last 4 st, k2tog, yo, k2.

ROW 4: K4, p to last 4 st, k4.

Rep rows 1–4 twice more—12 rows total.

Cont in St st with Eyelet Edge st and work 50 (56, 60, 60)

more rows—62 (68, 72, 72) rows total. Piece should meas 8¼ (9, 9½, 9½)"/20 (23, 24, 24)cm.

NEXT ROW (WS): Including Edge st, work 35 (40, 43, 47) sts, pm, work 28 (30,34,38) sts, pm, work to end.

BACK SHAPING:

NEXT ROW (RS): Work to 2 st before first marker, k2tog, slip marker, work to second marker, slip marker, ssk, work to end.

NEXT ROW: Work even.

Rep last 2 rows 6 (7, 7, 8) more times—84 (94, 104, 114) sts rem.

NEXT ROW: Work to first marker, m1r, slip marker, work to second marker, slip marker, m1l, work to end.

NEXT ROW: Work even.

Rep last 2 rows 4 (5, 6, 7) more times—94 (106, 118, 126) sts.

Work 3 (2, 5, 3) rows even in pats as est, then discontinue Eyelet Edge st.

Work 11 (14, 13, 15) more rows in St st. End after completing a WS row.

ARMHOLE SHAPING:

BO 5 (6, 7, 7) st at beg of next 2 rows.

NEXT ROW: Begin working Armhole Edge st, and AT THE SAME TIME, dec 2 sts inside Armhole Edge st at each end of next 0 (0, 1, 1) RS row,

then dec 1 st at each end of every RS row 5 (6, 6, 7) times—74 (82, 90, 100) sts rem.

Work 35 (39, 45, 43) rows even. End after completing a WS row.

NECKLINE SHAPING:

NEXT ROW: K16 (18, 20, 22) sts, attach a 2nd ball of yarn, and BO center 42 (46, 50, 56) sts. Knit to end.

Working both sides at the same time with reverse shaping, purl the next row, then dec 2 sts at each neck edge every RS row twice—12 (14, 16, 18) sts rem at each side.

Work 1 (1, 3, 3) rows even. BO.

ROUNDED HEMLINE:

Carefully remove crocheted chain and replace live 98 (110, 120, 132) sts on needle. Attach yarn so that you will be working a RS row.

ROW 1 (RS): K4, sssk, k to last 7 st, k3tog, k4.

ROW 2: K4, p to last 4 st, k4.

Cont to dec 2 sts at each end of every RS row 4 (5, 6, 6) more times.

Change to Garter st and work another 6 (7, 8, 8) rows, dec 2 sts at each end of every RS row—74 (82, 88, 100) sts rem. BO.

FRONT

Work first 12 rows same as for Back. After 12th row, continue in St st, working Eyelet Edge st.

Work 66 (74, 82, 82) more rows—78 (86, 94, 94) rows, 10 (11½, 12½, 12½)"/25 (29, 32, 32)cm total.

FRONT SHAPING:

NEXT ROW: Including Eyelet Edge st, work 33 (36, 40, 45) sts, s2kp, k28 (34, 36, 38), s2kp, k to end.

NEXT ROW AND FOLL 3 WS ROWS: Work Eyelet Edge st, p to last 4 sts, work Eyelet Edge st.

NEXT RS ROW: Work 31 (34, 38, 43), s2kp, k26 (32, 34, 36), s2kp, k to end.

NEXT RS ROW: Work 30 (33, 37, 42), s2kp, k24 (30, 32, 34), s2kp, k to end.

NEXT RS ROW: Work 29 (32, 36, 41), s2kp, k22 (28, 30, 32), s2kp, k to end—82 (94, 104, 116) sts rem.

Work 2 (2, 4, 4) rows even.

SIZE S ONLY: Discontinue Eyelet Edge st.

NEXT ROW: K29 (32, 36, 41), DLI, k22 (28 ,30, 32), DLI, k to end.

NEXT ROW: Purl.

NEXT ROW: K30 (33, 37, 42), s2kp, k24 (30, 32, 34), DLI, k to end.

SIZES M, L, XL ONLY: Discontinue Eyelet Edge st.

NEXT ROW: Purl.

NEXT ROW: K31 (34, 38, 43), s2kp, k26 (32, 34, 36), DLI, k to end—94 (106, 116, 128) sts.

Work 9 (9, 13, 17) rows even. End after completing a WS row.

ARMHOLE SHAPING:

BO 5 (6, 7, 7) st at beg of next 2 rows.

NEXT ROW: Start working Armhole Edge st, and AT THE SAME TIME, dec 2 sts inside the Armhole Edge st at each end of next RS row 0 (0, 1, 1) time, then dec 1 st at each end of the next 5 (6, 5, 5) RS rows—74 (82, 90, 100) sts rem.

Work 6 (6, 8, 8) rows even. End after completing a WS row.

NECKLINE SHAPING:

NEXT ROW: K29 (33, 36, 41) sts. Attach a 2nd ball of yarn, BO center 16 (16, 18, 18) sts, work to end.

Working both sides at the same time, dec 2 st at each neck edge every RS row 5 times, then dec 1 st at each neck edge every RS row twice, then every other RS row 5 (7, 7, 8) times—12 (14, 16, 18) sts rem in each shoulder.

Work 0 (0 ,2 ,0) rows even, or until Front meas same as Back at shoulders. BO all sts.

ROUNDED HEMLINE:

Work as for Back.

SIDE PANELS (MAKE 2)

Using the provisional cast-on method, CO 31 (33, 37, 37) sts.

Work the same as Back and Front for 5 rows, including Eyelet Edge st.

SIZE S ONLY: Dec 1 st each side of next row. Rep dec every 6 rows 7 more times, then every 8 rows 3 times. When it is time to dec from 11 to 9 sts, k4, s2kp, k4—9 sts rem.

SIZE M ONLY: Dec 1 st each side of next row. Rep dec every 6 rows another 6 times, then every 8 rows 5 times. When it is time to dec from 11 to 9 sts, this should also be an eyelet row. K2, yo, k2tog, s2kp, k2tog, yo, k2—9 sts rem.

SIZE L AND XL ONLY: Dec 1 st each side of next row. Rep dec every 6 rows another 9 times, then every 8 rows 4 times. When it is time to dec from 11 to 9 sts, k4, s2kp, k4—9 sts rem.

NEXT ROW (ALL SIZES): K4, p1, k4.

Work even for 4 rows.

NEXT ROW: K3, ssk, k2tog, k3—8 sts rem.

Knit 3 rows.

NEXT ROW: K2, ssk, k2tog, k2—6 sts rem.

Knit 3 rows.

THIS PROJECT WAS MADE WITH Elann's *Canapone*, 100% hemp, 1.75oz/50g = 180yd/165m per ball:

(A) 4 (4, 4, 5) balls, color Black

(B) 1 ball, color Cafe au Lait

NEXT ROW: K2, k2tog, k2—5 sts rem.

Knit 3 rows.

NEXT ROW: K1, sssk, k1—3 sts rem.

NEXT ROW: K3, then cut yarn, thread a tapestry needle, and draw yarn through rem 3 sts. Fasten off.

ROUNDED HEMLINE:

Work same as for Back and Front for 8 (10, 12, 12) rows—15 (13, 13, 13) sts rem on needle.

NEXT ROW: K4 (3, 3, 3), ssk, k1, k3tog, k4 (3, 3, 3)—11 (9, 9, 9) sts rem.

NEXT ROW: Knit.

NEXT ROW: K2 (1, 1, 1), ssk, k1, k3tog, k2 (1, 1, 1)—7 (5, 5, 5) sts rem.

NEXT ROW: Knit.

BO.

FINISHING

Steam block all pieces before assembling.

Sew shoulder and underarm seams using overcast method on the RS (this will create attractive cordlike seams and provide a little extra strength to the garment).

Single crochet around armhole

and neck edges.

Weave in ends. Due to the open nature of the knitted fabric, try to weave ends into the edge stitches as much as possible.

Steam again, paying particular attention to crocheted edging.

Lace up the sides or insert the panels the same way you'd lace a pair of sneakers, starting at the top and working your way down to the hem. The top eyelet of each panel is shared by both sides, and the last two eyelets on each edge are just for decoration. Threading the ribbon through a tapestry needle will make the job much easier.

CARE

Remove panels and hand wash pieces separately. Dry flat.

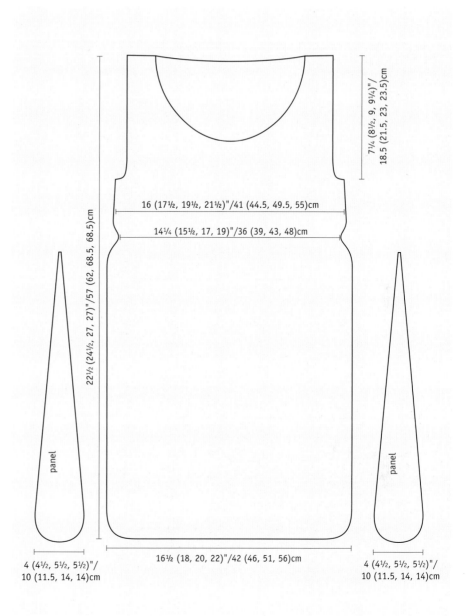

7¼ (8½, 9, 9¼)"/ 18.5 (21.5, 23, 23.5)cm

16 (17½, 19½, 21½)"/41 (44.5, 49.5, 55)cm

14¼ (15½, 17, 19)"/36 (39, 43, 48)cm

22½ (24½, 27, 27)"/57 (62, 68.5, 68.5)cm

panel

panel

4 (4½, 5½, 5½)"/ 10 (11.5, 14, 14)cm

16½ (18, 20, 22)"/42 (46, 51, 56)cm

4 (4½, 5½, 5½)"/ 10 (11.5, 14, 14)cm

An elegant tunic with bell-shaped sleeves and a wraparound side tie closure, the design was named after a good friend who gave the designer a frank and honest opinion on what she loved and hated about the maternity clothes she recently wore.

anne's tunic

DESIGN BY **LINDSAY OBERMEYER**

EXPERIENCE LEVEL

INTERMEDIATE

SIZE S (M, L, XL)

FINISHED MEASUREMENTS

BUST: 38 (40, 42, 44)"/97 (102, 107, 112)cm

LENGTH: 26 (26, 28, 28)"/66 (66, 71, 71)cm

NOTE: Adjust length as desired for a more personal fit.

materials

APPROX TOTAL: 1202 (1276, 1404, 1527)yd/1099 (1167, 1284, 1396)m

COLOR A: 1127 (1176, 1274, 1372)yd/1031 (1075, 1165, 1255)m of extra fine merino wool in light brown

COLOR B: 75 (100, 130, 155)yd/ 68 (91, 119, 142)m of mohair/silk blend in light grey

KNITTING NEEDLES:

4.5mm (size 7 U.S.) circular needle 24"/61cm long *or size to obtain gauge*

4.5mm (size 7 U.S.), 2 double-pointed needles

CROCHET HOOK: 3.75mm (size F-5 U.S.)

Tapestry needle

gauge

18 sts and 26 rows = 4"/10cm over St st

Always take time to check your gauge.

pattern stitches

STOCKINETTE STITCH

ROW 1 (RS): Knit.

ROW 2 (WS): Purl.

Rep rows 1 and 2 for pat.

I-CORD

ALL ROWS: Knit all sts, do not turn. Slide sts to other end of dpn.

instructions

BACK

With color A and circular needle, CO 96 (100, 104, 108) sts.

Begin working in St st.

Dec 1 st each side every 17 (17, 18, 19) rows until 86 (90, 94, 98) sts rem.

Work in St st for another 3 (3, 4, 4)"/7.6 (7.6, 10, 10)cm. End after completing a WS row.

SHAPE ARMHOLES:

NOTE: Right armhole dec should be worked as a ssk and left armhole as a k2tog.

BO 5 sts at beg of next 2 rows, then dec 1 st on each edge of the next 4 RS rows—68 (72, 76, 80) sts rem.

Work even until armhole meas 9 (9, 10, 10)"/23 (23, 25, 25)cm.

BEGIN NECK AND SHOULDER SHAPING:

K20 (21, 23, 25) sts, add a 2nd ball of yarn and BO center 28 (30, 30, 30) sts, k20 (21, 23, 25) sts to end.

Working both sides AT THE SAME TIME, BO 2 sts on each neck edge 2 times, and AT THE

Dec 1 st 4 times every other row on RS using a k2tog.

When only 16 (17, 19, 21) sts rem and armhole meas 9 (9, 10, 10)"/23 (23, 25, 25)cm, beg shoulder shaping.

SHOULDER SHAPING:

BO 3 (4, 5, 5) sts on left edge 3 times.

BO rem 7 (5, 4, 6) sts.

RIGHT FRONT

With color A and circular needle, CO 64 (68, 72, 76) sts.

Begin working in St st.

Dec 1 st on right edge every 17 (17, 18, 19) rows until 59 (63, 67, 71) sts rem. End after completing a RS row.

Cont working right edge even until piece meas same as back to armhole. Beg neck shaping on left edge immediately after last dec on right edge.

NECK SHAPING:

✳ **NOTE:** On RS work dec as a k2tog and work dec on WS as an p2tog.

Dec 1 st at neck edge of next 12 rows—47 (51, 55, 59) sts rem.

Cont working dec 1 st on RS rows only.

AT THE SAME TIME, when piece meas same as Back to armhole, beg armhole shaping.

ARMHOLE SHAPING:

BO 5 sts on left edge.

SAME TIME, BO 3 (4, 5, 5) sts at shoulder edge 3 times.

BO rem 7 (5, 4, 6) sts on each shoulder.

LEFT FRONT

With color A and circular needle, CO 64 (68, 72, 76) sts.

Begin working in St st.

Dec 1 st on left edge every 17 (17, 18, 19) rows until 59 (63, 67, 71) sts rem. End after completing a RS row.

EYELET BUTTONHOLE:

NEXT ROW (WS): Purl.

NEXT ROW (RS): K until 10 sts rem on left needle, K2tog, yo twice, ssk, knit rem sts.

NEXT ROW: P all stitches including yarn overs.

Cont working left edge even for next 3"/8cm (approx 20 rows) until Front meas same as Back to armhole, and AT THE SAME TIME, beg neck shaping on right edge immediately after last dec on left edge.

NECK SHAPING:

✳ **NOTE:** On RS work dec as an ssk and on WS p2tog-tbl.

Dec 1 st at neck edge of next 12 rows—47 (51, 55, 59) sts rem.

Cont working dec 1 st on RS rows only.

AT THE SAME TIME, when piece meas same as Back to armhole, beg armhole shaping.

ARMHOLE SHAPING:

BO 5 sts left edge.

Dec 1 st 4 times every other row on RS using an ssk.

When only 16 (17, 19, 21) sts rem and armhole meas 9 (9, 10, 10)"/23 (23, 25, 25)cm, beg shoulder shaping.

SHOULDER SHAPING:

BO 3 (4, 5, 5) sts on right edge 3 times.

BO rem 7 (5, 4, 6) sts.

SLEEVES (MAKE 2)

With color A and circular needle, CO 58 (64, 68, 72) sts.

Dec 1 st every 19 (9, 10, 11) rows on each edge 2 (5, 5, 5) times—54 (54, 58, 62) sts remain.

Inc 1 st every 5 (5, 4, 5) rows on each edge 12 (12, 16, 14) times—78 (78, 90, 90) sts, continue in St st until sleeve meas 16 (17, 19, 20)"/41 (43, 48, 51)cm from CO. End after completing a WS row.

CAP SHAPING:

BO 5 sts at beg of next 2 rows.

Dec 1 st every RS row on each

edge 15 (15, 17, 17) times— 38 (38, 46, 46) sts rem and cap meas approx 6 (6, 7, 7)"/15 (15, 18, 18)cm.

BO 3 (3, 5, 5) sts at beg of next 2 rows, then BO 2 sts at beg of next 2 rows—28 (28, 32, 32) sts rem.

BO rem sts.

CUFF TRIM:

With color B pick up 58 (64, 68, 72) sts at the CO edge.

Starting on WS, work in St st for 7 rows.

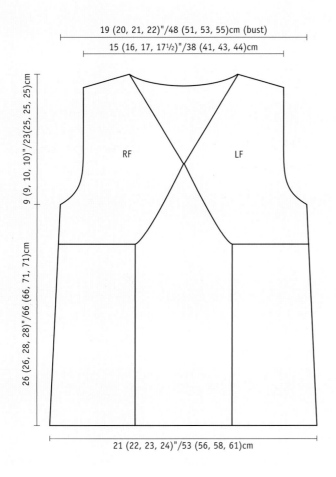

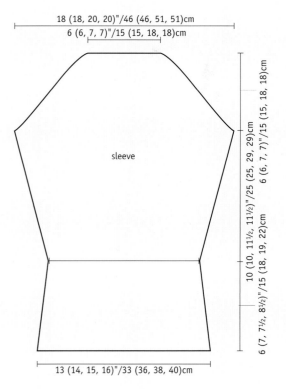

NEXT ROW (RS): *K2tog, yo*; rep from * to *, end k1.

Work in St st for another 7 rows.

BO all stitches loosely using larger needle.

Fold trim in half and sew into place.

FINISHING

Weave in all ends. Sew shoulder seams. Set in Sleeves. Sew arm and side seams. Weave ends.

PICOT KNIT TRIM ON NECKLINE:

With color B pick up 138 (142, 146, 150) sts along the left side starting at the bottom edge, pick up another 77 sts along the back, and the final 40 (45, 49, 54) sts along the right edge, ending at base of right side dec—255 (264, 272, 281) sts total.

Starting on WS work in St st for 7 rows.

ROW 8 (RS): *K2tog, yo*; rep from *to* to last st, k1.

Work in St st for another 7 rows.

BO loosely.

Fold trim in half and sew into place.

Work Medium Picot crochet trim along hem and right front side edge using crochet hook and color A as foll: *make 3 chain sts, make 1 sc in first of the 3 chains, skip 1 st on the edge of the knitting, then make 1 sc in the next knitted st. Rep from * until entire edge is complete.

CORD:

CO 6 sts.

Work I-cord for 56"/142cm.

Attach to right front at base of neck dec.

Work 2nd I-cord for 16"/41cm.

Attach to left front at base of neck dec.

Weave in ends.

To tie the sweater, run right front cord through eyelet buttonhole and around the back. Tie in a bow with left front cord.

THIS PROJECT WAS MADE WITH

(A) 12 (12, 13, 14) balls of Karabella Yarns' *Aurora 8*, 100% extra fine merino wool, 1.75oz/50g = approx 98yd/90m, color #1362

(B) 1 (1, 1, 1) ball of Rowan's *Kidsilk Night*, 67% super kid mohair/18% silk/10% polyester/5% nylon, .88oz/25g = 227yd/208m, color #608 Moonlight

Style secret: this cabled shrug (the fashion-obsessed's name for "super-short") hangs high above the tummy—so much so that it can be worn throughout every stage of pregnancy, and beyond.

cabled shrug hoodie

DESIGN BY **STAR ATHENA**

EXPERIENCE LEVEL

INTERMEDIATE

SIZE S (M, L, XL)

FINISHED MEASUREMENTS

Approx 49 (50, 52, 52½)"/ 125 (127, 132, 133)cm cuff to cuff, blocked, including ribbed edging

materials

540 (648, 648, 756)yd/ 494 (593, 593, 691)m alpaca/tencel blend DK weight yarn

KNITTING NEEDLES: 3.75mm (size 5 U.S.) circular needle 32"/81cm long *or size to obtain gauge*

Cable needle

Tapestry needle for sewing seams

gauge

23 sts and 28 rows = 4"/10cm in St st

Always take time to check your gauge.

pattern stitch

K2, P2 RIB

ALL ROWS: (K2, p2) across.

instructions

✳ **NOTE:** The shrug is knit up from the left Sleeve, across the Back, and down the right Sleeve. The cable is designed to run across the top of the back. The Hood is worked by picking up stitches, and finishes with Kitchener stitch for a smooth seam on the top of the head. Even though the garment is knit with circular needles, the piece is worked flat and seamed. The pattern is easily customizable, so take the time to measure your arms and back first—that way you can get an exact fit!

LEFT SLEEVE

LEFT CUFF:

CO 64 (64, 68, 72) sts.

Work in K2, P2 Rib for 2"/5cm or desired cuff length.

LEFT SLEEVE SHAPING:

ROW 1 (RS): K18 (18, 20, 22), work row 1 of Cable Chart over next 16 sts, k30 (30, 32, 34).

ROW 2 (WS): P30 (30, 32, 34), work row 2 of chart over next 16 sts, p18 (18, 20, 22).

ROW 3 (DEC ROW): K1, ssk, work in pats as est to last 3 sts, k2tog, k1—62 (62, 66, 70) sts.

Cont in pats as est, and dec as above every 4 rows twice— 58 (58, 62, 66) sts.

Work even for 5 (5, 7, 9) rows.

LEFT SLEEVE SHAPING:

NEXT ROW (INC ROW): K1, m1, work in pats as est to last st, m1, k1.

Cont working pats as est, and inc as above every 20 rows until you have 68 (68, 72, 76) sts.

Work even until Sleeve meas 17 (17, 17½, 17½)"/43 (43, 44, 44)cm or desired length to armhole. End after completing a WS row.

LEFT ARMHOLE SHAPING:

Continue pats as est and shape as foll:

ROW 1 (RS): BO 1 st at beg.

ROW 2 (WS): BO 3 sts at beg.

ROW 3: Dec 1 st at beg.

ROW 4: Dec 2 sts at beg.

ROW 5: Dec 1 st at end.

ROW 6: Dec 1 st at beg.

ROW 7: Dec 1 st at beg, dec 2 sts at end.

ROW 8: Dec 2 sts at beg.

ROW 9: Dec 1 st at beg, dec 2sts at end.

ROW 10: Dec 1 st at beg.

ROW 11: Dec 2 sts at end.

ROW 12: Dec 1 st at beg.

ROW 13: Dec 2 sts at end.

ROW 14: Work even.

ROW 15: Dec 2 sts at end.

ROW 16: Work even.

ROW 17: Dec 2 sts at end.

ROW 18: Work even.

ROW 19: Dec 2 sts at end.

ROW 20: Work even.

ROW 21: Dec 2 sts at end.

ROW 22: Work even.

ROW 23: Dec 2 sts at end.

ROW 24: Work even—33 (33, 37, 41) sts rem for Back.

BACK

Work even in pats as est until Back meas 15 (16, 17, 17½)"/38 (41, 43, 45)cm or desired length from shoulder to shoulder.

RIGHT ARMHOLE SHAPING:

ROW 1 (RS): Inc 2 sts at end.

ROW 2 (WS): Work even.

ROW 3: Inc 2 sts at end.

ROW 4: Work even.

ROW 5: Inc 2 sts at end.

ROW 6: Work even.

ROW 7: Inc 2 sts at end.

ROW 8: Work even.

ROW 9: Inc 2 sts at end.

ROW 10: Work even.

ROW 11: Inc 2 sts at end.

ROW 12: Inc 1 st at beg.

ROW 13: Inc 2 sts at end.

ROW 14: Inc 1 st at beg.

ROW 15: Inc 1 st at beg, inc 2 sts at end.

ROW 16: Inc 2 sts at beg.

ROW 17: Inc 1 st at beg, inc 2 sts at end.

ROW 18: Inc 1 st at beg.

ROW 19: Inc 1 st at end.

ROW 20: Inc 2 sts at beg.

ROW 21: Inc 1 st at beg.

ROW 22: CO 3 sts at beg.

ROW 23: CO 1 st at beg— 68 (68, 72, 76) sts.

Work even for 3 (3, 5, 7) rows.

RIGHT SLEEVE SHAPING:

ROW 1 (DEC ROW): K1, ssk, work in pats as est to last 3 sts, k2tog, k1.

Cont in pats as est, working dec every 20 rows until you have 58 (58, 62, 66) sts.

Work even until sleeve meas 15 (15, 15½, 15½)"/38 (38, 39, 39)cm or desired length to cuff.

CHART A

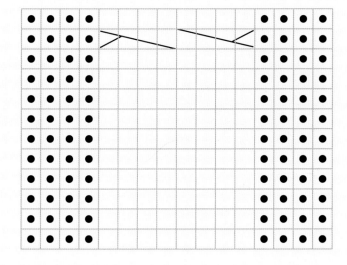

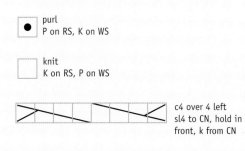

• purl
P on RS, K on WS

☐ knit
K on RS, P on WS

c4 over 4 left
sl4 to CN, hold in front, k from CN

RIGHT CUFF:

Work in K2, P2 rib for 2"/5cm or desired cuff length. BO in rib pat.

HOOD

Find back center of shrug and, using circular needle, pick up 40 (42, 44, 46) sts along right shoulder, pm, pick up center st, pm, Pick up 40 (42, 44, 46) sts along left shoulder.

 NOTE: Pick up 5 sts for every 6 sts on shrug.

Work in St st for 1 (1½, 1½, 2)"/2.5 (4, 4, 5)cm.

Inc 1 st each side of center back st every other row 7 times—95 (99,103, 107) sts.

Work even until Hood measures 9½ (9½, 10, 10)"/24 (24, 25, 25)cm from pick-up row, end with a RS row.

HOOD TOP SHAPING:

NEXT ROW (RS): Work to 1 st before center st, k2tog, work to end.

Work 1 row even.

NEXT ROW: Remove 2 markers and place a new marker at the center back to divide the sts in half.

Dec 2 sts (using k3tog) on each side of the center marker on next row, then every other row 4 times more. Divide rem sts on two separate needles and join using Kitchener st.

FINISHING

Seam Sleeves and block garment. Weave in ends.

HOOD EDGING:

Using circular needle, starting at the top of the right sleeve, 1 (1½, 1½, 2)"/3 (4, 4, 5)cm from seam, pick up 172 (176, 184, 188) sts evenly along the shoulder, around the Hood, and back down left Sleeve, stopping at the same point you started on the right Sleeve. Work K2, P2 Rib for 2 rows. Then, dec 1 st at beg and 1 st at end for 2 rows 168 (172, 180, 184) sts.

NEXT ROW: Dec 2 sts at beg and 2 sts at end—164 (168, 176, 180) sts.

Dec 2 sts at beg, dec 2 sts where Hood meets right shoulder, dec 2 sts where Hood meets left shoulder, dec 2 sts at end for 3 rows—140 (144, 152, 156) sts.

BO in Rib pat.

BACK EDGING:

Using circular needle, starting at the bottom of the left Sleeve at the seam, pick up 104 (108, 112, 116) sts evenly across the Back. Work K2, P2 Rib for 2 rows. Then, dec 1 st at beg and 1 st at end for 2 rows—100 (104, 108, 112) sts.

Dec 2 sts at beg and 2 sts at end for 4 rows—84 (88, 92, 96) sts.

BO in Rib pat. Weave in rem ends.

THIS PROJECT WAS MADE WITH 5 (6, 6, 7) skeins of Classic Elite Yarns' *Miracle*, 50% alpaca/50% tencel yarn, 1.75 oz/50g = 108 yd/99m per skein, color #3385

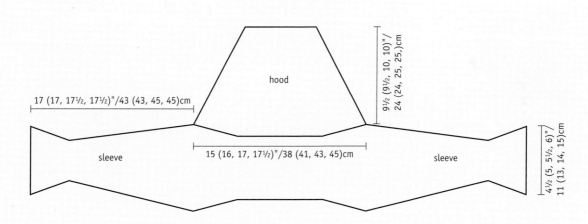

Because this tunic is knit in a stretchy, ribbed fabric, the sizing can be more flexible than most. Choose the size that's best for either a closer or looser fit and how much smocking you want to do. To lengthen the three-quarter sleeve just purchase an extra skein of yarn.

river tunic

DESIGN BY **CHER UNDERWOOD FORSBERG**

EXPERIENCE LEVEL

INTERMEDIATE

SIZE S (M, L, XL)

FINISHED MEASUREMENTS

Bust: 34½ (38½, 42½, 46¾)"/88 (98, 108, 119)cm

materials

1320 (1430, 1540, 1650)yd/ 1207 (1308, 1408, 1509)m of sport-weight cotton/modal blend yarn in blue

KNITTING NEEDLES: 3.75mm (size 5 U.S.) circular needle 24"/61cm long

3.75mm (size 5 U.S.) double-pointed needles

Stitch markers

Stitch holders

gauge

24 sts and 34 rows = 4"/10cm over Twisted Rib Pattern

Always take time to check your gauge.

pattern stitches

Worked over a multiple of 4 sts.

TWISTED RIB PATTERN (CIRCULAR)

ALL RNDS: *P3, k1 tbl;* rep to end of round.

TWISTED RIB PATTERN (BACK AND FORTH)

ROW 1 (RS): *P3, k1 tbl;* rep to end of row.

ROW 2 (WS): *K3, p1 tbl;* rep to end of row.

Rep rows 1 and 2 for pat.

instructions

LOWER BODY

Using circular needle, CO 228 (252, 280, 308) sts. Join to work in the round, being careful not to twist sts.

RND 1: Pm, work Twisted Rib over 114 (126, 140, 154) sts, pm, work Twisted Rib to end of rnd.

Work even for 4 (3, 1, 1) rnd(s), slipping markers as you come to them.

DEC ROUND: *Knit to 2 sts before marker, ssk, slip marker, k2tog;* rep from * to *.

Rep dec rnd every 29 (30, 25, 21) rounds 4 (4, 5, 6) times—208 (232, 256, 280) sts rem.

Work even until piece meas 17½ (18, 18½, 18¾)"/45 (46, 47, 48)cm from beg.

DIVIDE FOR ARMHOLE:

Remove marker at beg of round, slip 104 (116, 128, 140) sts to a st holder for the Front, remove 2nd marker.

UPPER BACK

BO 4 (5, 6, 6) sts at beg of next 2 rows. Dec 1 st at each end of every RS row 8 (10, 13, 15) times—80 (86, 90, 98) sts rem.

Work even until armhole meas 4¾ (5, 5¼, 5½)"/12 (13, 13, 14)cm.

BACK NECK SHAPING:

Cont in pat, work 28 (30, 32, 35) sts. Sl 24 (26, 26, 28) sts to a holder. Join a 2nd ball of yarn and work rem 28 (30, 32, 35) sts. Dec 1 st at neck edge every row 11 (12, 13, 15) times—17 (18, 19, 20) sts rem.

Work even until armhole meas 7¾ (8¼, 8¾, 9¼)"/20 (21, 22, 24)cm.

End right shoulder after completing a WS row. End left shoulder after completing a RS row.

RIGHT SHOULDER SHAPING:

NEXT ROW (RS): Work 12 (13, 14, 15) sts, W&T.

NEXT ROW (AND ALL WS ROWS): P to end.

NEXT RS ROW: Work 8 (8, 9, 10) sts, W&T.

NEXT RS ROW: Work 4 (4, 4, 5) sts, W&T.

NEXT RS ROW: Work 17 (18, 19, 20) sts, picking up wraps as you come to them and knitting them with the st they

are wrapped around. Slip all sts to a holder.

LEFT SHOULDER SHAPING:

NEXT ROW (WS): Work 12 (13, 14, 15) sts, W&T.

NEXT ROW (AND ALL RS ROWS): P to end.

NEXT WS ROW: Work 8 (8, 9, 10) sts, W&T.

NEXT WS ROW: Work 4 (4, 4, 5) sts, W&T.

NEXT WS ROW: Work 17 (18, 19, 20) sts, picking up wraps as you come to them and knitting them with the st they are wrapped around. Slip all sts to a holder.

UPPER FRONT

Slip sts back to working needles. Work as given for Back until armhole meas 3¼ (3½, 3½, 3¾)"/8 (9, 9, 10)cm.

NECK SHAPING:

Work 32 (35, 36, 40) sts. Slip the next 16 (16, 18, 18) sts to a holder. Joining a 2nd ball of yarn, work rem 32 (35, 36, 40) sts. Dec 1 st at neck edge every row 7 (8, 8, 10) times, then every RS row 8 (9, 9, 10) times—17 (18, 19, 20) sts rem.

Work even until armhole meas 7¾ (8¼, 8¾, 9¼)"/20 (21, 22, 24)cm.

Shape shoulders as for back.

Join shoulders using the three-needle bind off.

SLEEVES (MAKE 2)

With dpns, pick up 68 (72, 80, 84) sts around armhole.

Begin working in Twisted Rib pat, and AT THE SAME TIME shape sleeve cap as foll:

ROW 1 (RS): Work 45 (48, 53, 56) sts; turn work.

ROW 2 (WS): Work 22 (24, 26, 28) sts; turn work.

ROW 3: Work 23 (25, 27, 29) sts; turn work.

ROW 4: Work 24 (26, 28, 30) sts; turn work.

Cont in this fashion, working one more st on every row until all 68 (72, 80, 84) sts have been knit. Place marker and beg working in the round.

DEC ROUND: K2tog, work to last 2 sts of round, ssk.

Rep dec rnd every 13 (14, 12, 10) rounds 4 (3, 2, 4) times, then every 11 (11, 18, 11) rounds 0 (1, 2, 0) times—58 (62, 70, 74) sts rem.

Work even until Sleeve meas 13½ (14, 14½, 15)"/34 (36, 37, 38)cm. BO loosely.

FINISHING

SMOCKING:

Using the photo as a guide, add smocking to upper body of sweater using a tapestry needle and yarn:

1. Beginning with the 2nd knit rib at the armhole, bring the needle from the WS to the RS

of the fabric through the center of the knit stitch.

2. *Insert the needle from right to left into the same stitch on the 1st and 2nd ribs. Pull the yarn tight to draw the ribs together. Rep from * once.

3. *Insert the needle from left to right 13 rows up, on the 2nd and 3rd ribs. Pull the yarn tight to draw the ribs together. Rep from * once.

Rep steps 2 and 3 until all of the upper body is smocked, as shown in figure 1.

COLLAR:

Pick up and knit 160 (172, 184, 196) sts evenly around neckline. Knit 6 rows. BO loosely. Weave in ends.

SMOCKING (figure 1)

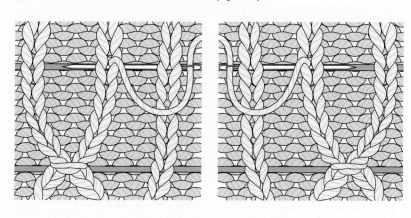

THIS SWEATER WAS MADE WITH 12 (13, 14, 15) skeins of Knit Picks' *Shine Sport*, 60% pima cotton/40% modal, 1.75oz/50g = 110yd/101m per skein, color #23622 River

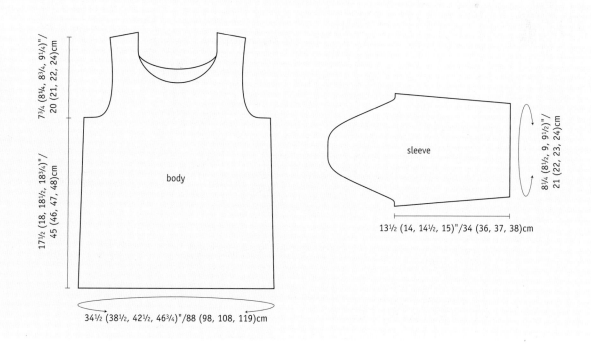

A sleek and simple mock turtleneck tunic trimmed with cable ribbing says you and TAFKAP are as one (just don't tell your husband). Two sets of short-row shaping at the belly help keep it from riding up in front.

purple rain sleeveless tunic

DESIGN BY **MELISSA WEHRLE**

EXPERIENCE LEVEL

INTERMEDIATE

SIZE S (M, L, XL)

FINISHED MEASUREMENTS

BUST: 37 (39, 43, 45)"/94 (99, 109, 114)cm

LENGTH: 29½ (30, 30½, 31)"/ 75 (76, 77, 79)cm

materials

780 (850, 920, 975)yd/713 (777, 841, 892)m of silk/cotton blend worsted weight yarn in fuchsia

KNITTING NEEDLES: 5mm (size 8 U.S.) circular needle 24"/61cm long or longer, *or size to obtain gauge*

4.5mm (size 7 U.S.) circular needle 24"/61cm long or longer

4mm (size 6 U.S.) circular needle 16"/41cm long

2 stitch holders

gauge

16 sts and 22 rows = 4"/10cm over St st using larger needles

Always take time to check your gauge.

pattern stitches

CABLE RIBBING

Worked over a multiple of 4 + 2 sts.

ROWS 1 AND 3 (WS): K2, *p2, k2; rep from * to end.

ROW 2 (RS): P2, *k2, p2; rep from * to end.

ROW 4: P2, * k2tog, leaving both sts on needle, then insert right-hand needle between the 2 sts knitted together and knit the 1st st again; sl both sts off needle, p2, rep from *.

Rep rows 1–4 for pat.

K1, P1 RIBBING (CIRCULAR)

ALL RNDS: *K1, p1; rep from* around.

ARMHOLE AND NECK EDGING ST

ROW 1 (RS): Sl1 wyif, p1, k1, p1, work to last 4 sts, p1, k1, p1, k1.

ROW 2 (WS): Sl1 wyif, k1, p1, k1, work to last 4 sts, k1, p1, k1, p1.

Rep rows 1 and 2 for pat.

STOCKINETTE STITCH

ROW 1 (RS): Knit.

ROW 2: Purl.

Rep rows 1 and 2 for pat.

instructions

BACK

With smaller 24"/61cm circular needle, CO 82 (86, 94, 98) sts.

Work in Cable Ribbing for 4"/10cm. End after completing a WS row.

STOCKINETTE STITCH

ROW 1 (RS): Knit.

ROW 2: Purl.

Rep rows 1 and 2 for pat.

DEC ROW (RS): K1, ssk, work to last 3 sts, k2tog, k1.

Rep dec row every 4 rows 5 times more—70 (74, 82, 86) sts.

Work 9 rows even. End after completing a WS row.

INC ROW (RS): Kf/b, work to last 2 sts, kf/b, k1.

Repeat inc row every 24 rows 1 time more—74 (78, 86, 90) sts.

Work even until Back meas 20¾ (21¼, 21¼, 21¼)"/ 53 (54, 54, 54)cm. End after completing a WS row.

ARMHOLE SHAPING:

Beg working Armhole and Neck Edging st, and AT THE SAME TIME, BO 5 (5, 6, 7) sts at beg of next 2 rows, then dec 1 st at each edge every row 4 times, then dec every other row 1 (2, 3, 3) times—54 (56, 60, 62) sts.

Work even in pat as est until armhole meas 7½ (7¾, 8, 8½)"/19 (20, 20, 22)cm. End after completing a WS row.

NECK AND SHOULDER SHAPING:

Continue working Armhole and Neck Edging st and, and AT THE SAME TIME, BO 3 (3, 4, 4) sts at armhole edge, work across until there are 12 (12, 13, 14) sts on right-hand needle. Turn and place remaining sts on holder.

NEXT ROW (WS): P1, p2tog, work to end of row.

NEXT ROW (RS): BO 3 (3, 4, 4) sts at armhole edge, work to last 3 sts, k2tog, k1.

NEXT ROW: P1, p2tog, work to end of row.

NEXT ROW: BO 3 (3, 4, 4) sts at armhole edge.

Work 1 row even. BO rem 3 (3, 2, 3) sts.

Rejoin yarn, leaving 24 (26, 26, 26) center back sts on holder, work across row to end.

NEXT ROW (WS): BO 3 (3, 4, 4) sts at armhole edge, work to last 3 sts, ssp, p1.

NEXT ROW (RS): K1, ssk, work to end of row.

NEXT ROW: BO 3 (3, 4, 4) sts at armhole edge, work to last 3 sts, ssp, p1.

Work 1 row even. BO 3 (3, 4, 4) sts at beg of next row.

Work 1 row even. BO rem 3 (3, 2, 3) sts.

FRONT

With smaller 24"/61cm circular needle, CO 82 (86, 94, 98) sts.

Work in Cable Ribbing for 4"/10cm. End after completing a WS row.

Change to larger 24"/61cm circular needle and work even in St st until front meas 9"/23cm. End after completing a WS row.

SHORT ROW SHAPING (1ST SET):

ROW 1 (RS): K across to last 5 (5, 6, 6) sts, W&T.

ROW 2 (WS): P across to last 5 (5, 6, 6) sts, W&T.

ROW 3: K across to last 10 (10, 12, 12) sts, W&T.

ROW 4: P across to last 10 (10, 12, 12) sts, W&T.

ROW 5: K across to last 15 (15, 18, 18) sts, W&T.

ROW 6: P across to last 15 (15, 18, 18) sts, W&T.

ROW 7: K across to last 20 (20, 24, 24) sts, W&T.

ROW 8: P across to last 20 (20, 24, 24) sts, W&T.

ROW 9: K to end of row, when you encounter a wrapped st, pick up the wrap and place it on the left needle, then k it tog with the wrapped st.

ROW 10: P. Pick up each rem wrap and p it tog with the wrapped st.

Work even until Front meas 10"/25cm from beg. End after completing a WS row.

DEC ROW (RS): K1, ssk, work to last 3 sts, k2tog, k1.

Rep dec row every 4 rows 5 more times—70 (74, 82, 86) sts.

AT THE SAME TIME, when Front meas 12½"/32cm from the beg, end after completing a WS row and beg 2nd set of short row shaping as foll.

SHORT ROW SHAPING (2ND SET):

ROW 1 (RS): K to last 4 (4, 5, 5) sts, W&T.

ROW 2 (WS): P to last 4 (4, 5, 5) sts, W&T.

ROW 3: K to last 8 (8, 10, 10) sts, W&T.

ROW 4: P to last 8 (8, 10, 10) sts, W&T.

ROW 5: K to last 12 (12, 15, 15) sts, W&T.

ROW 6: P to last 12 (12, 15, 15) sts, W&T.

ROW 7: K to last 16 (16, 20, 20) sts, W&T.

ROW 8: P to last 16 (16, 20, 20) sts, W&T.

ROW 9: K to end of row, when you encounter a wrapped st, pick up the wrap and place it on the left needle, then k it tog with the wrapped st.

ROW 10: P. Pick up each rem wrap and p it tog with the wrapped st.

When Front meas 14 ½"/37cm from beg, work 9 rows even, ending after completing a WS row.

Inc row (RS): Kf/b, work to last 2 sts, kf/b, k1.

Rep inc row every 24 rows once more—74 (78, 86, 90) sts.

Work even until Front meas same as Back to armhole. End after completing a WS row.

ARMHOLE SHAPING:

BO 5 (5, 6, 7) sts at beg of next 2 rows. Dec 1 st at each edge every row 4 times, then every other row 1 (2, 3, 3) times—54 (56, 60, 62) sts.

AT THE SAME TIME, when Front meas 27½ (28, 28½, 29)"/ 70 (71, 72, 74)cm start neck shaping.

NECK SHAPING:

Work across 22 (22, 24, 25) sts, place 10 (12, 12, 12) sts on holder. Join 2nd ball of yarn and work to end of row.

Working both sides AT THE SAME TIME, BO 2 sts at neck edge every other row 1 time and then dec 1 st at neck edge every row 8 times.

AT THE SAME TIME, when armhole meas 7½ (7¾, 8, 8½)"/19 (20, 20, 22)cm, ending on a WS row on the Left Front and ending on a RS row on the Right Front, start shoulder shaping.

SHOULDER SHAPING:

Working both shoulders AT THE SAME TIME, BO 3 (3, 4, 4) sts at beg of next row. Work 1 row even. Rep last 2 rows 2 more times. BO rem 3 (3, 2, 3) sts.

FINISHING

Block pieces to measurements. Sew shoulder seams and side seams.

MOCK NECK:

With RS facing and 16"/41cm circular needle, pick up and knit 7 sts from right back neck, 24 (26, 26, 26) from back neck holder, 7 sts from left back neck, 19 sts from left front neck, 10 (12, 12, 12) sts from front holder, and 19 sts from right front neck—86 (90, 90, 90) sts. Work in K1, P1 Ribbing for 3"/8cm. Using tubular bind off, BO all sts.

THIS PROJECT WAS MADE WITH 7 (8, 8, 9) skeins of Rowan's *Summer Tweed*, 70% silk/30% cotton, 1.5oz/50g = 118yd/108m per skein, color #528 Brilliant

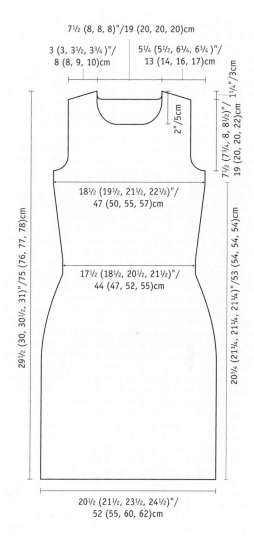

7½ (8, 8, 8)"/19 (20, 20, 20)cm

3 (3, 3½, 3¾)"/ 8 (8, 9, 10)cm

5¼ (5½, 6¼, 6¾)"/ 13 (14, 16, 17)cm

1¼"/3cm

2"/5cm

7½ (7¾, 8, 8½)"/ 19 (20, 20, 22)cm

18½ (19½, 21½, 22½)"/ 47 (50, 55, 57)cm

17½ (18½, 20½, 21½)"/ 44 (47, 52, 55)cm

29½ (30, 30½, 31)"/75 (76, 77, 78)cm

20¾ (21¼, 21¼, 21¼)"/53 (54, 54, 54)cm

20½ (21½, 23½, 24½)"/ 52 (55, 60, 62)cm

This hot number has a clever knot in the front yoke that causes the skirt to drape dramatically into an asymmetrical hemline. Still more pleats, on the shoulders, complete the whole look.

red twist dress

DESIGN BY **HELEN HAMANN**

instructions

The yoke of this garment is worked in one piece from side to side, beginning with the back, continuing with the right front, and ending with the left front. (See illustration on page 104.)

BACK

With waste yarn, use provisional cast on and CO 90 (96, 100) sts.

ROW 1 (RS): Change to main yarn and k42 (46, 46) sts.

Work in St st on these sts only for 3 more rows.

LEFT ARMHOLE SHAPING:

ROW 1 (RS): K44 (48, 48), W&T.

ROW 2 (AND ALL WS ROWS): P to end.

ROW 3: K to last wrapped st, k next st tog with its wrap, k1, W&T.

ROW 5: K all 90 (96, 100) sts from provisional CO.

Work even in St st for 116 (132, 146) rows or until piece meas 15 (17, 19)"/38 (43, 48)cm on shorter edge. End after working a WS row.

RIGHT ARMHOLE SHAPING:

ROW 1 (RS): K46 (52,52), W&T.

ROW 2 (AND ALL WS ROWS): P to end.

ROW 3: K44 (50, 50), W&T.

ROW 5: K42 (46, 46) with main yarn and k rem sts with waste yarn.

NEXT ROW: Work with waste yarn the sts worked on previous row and cont the sts with main yarn.

Work rem 42 (46, 46) sts for 3 more rows.

EXPERIENCE LEVEL
EXPERIENCED

SIZE S (M, L)

FINISHED MEASUREMENTS

BUST: 36 (40, 44)"/91 (102, 112)cm

SKIRT LENGTH: 25"/64cm (all sizes)

materials

2298 (2398, 2507)yd/ 2093 (2193, 2292)m worsted weight alpaca yarn in burgundy

KNITTING NEEDLES: 4mm (size 6 U.S.) circular needles 32"/81cm and 16"/41cm long, and double-pointed needles, *or size to obtain gauge*

Tapestry needle

Stitch markers

A few yards (meters) of waste yarn and smooth, satin ribbon for provisional cast on

Stitch holders

gauge

20 sts and 29 rows = 4"/10cm over St st

pattern stitches

STOCKINETTE STITCH

ROW 1 (RS): Knit.

ROW 2 (WS): Purl.

Rep rows 1 and 2 for pat.

GARTER STITCH

Knit every stitch in every row.

RIGHT FRONT

ARMHOLE SHAPING:

ROW 1 (RS): K42 (46,46), W&T.

ROW 2 (AND ALL WS ROWS): P to end.

ROW 3: K to last wrapped st, k next st tog with its wrap, k1, W&T.

Transfer rem sts on waste yarn to a stitch holder.

Work even for 138 (154, 168) rows. Transfer sts to holder.

LEFT FRONT

With extra needle, pick up 42 (46, 46) sts from provisional CO and work as for Right Front, working short rows at shoulder edge to shape armhole.

LEFT SLEEVE

With working needle and open sts from Left Front still on needle, pick up the rem provisional CO 48 (50, 50) sts, placing a marker at shoulder.

CAP SHAPING:

NEXT ROW (RS): K to 16 sts after shoulder marker, wrap next st and turn. P to 16 sts after shoulder marker, W&T. *K to 6 sts after last wrapped st, working the wrap tog with the wrapped st. P to 6 sts after last wrapped st, working the wrap tog with the wrapped st.* Rep from * to * one more time. **K to 4 sts after last wrapped st, working the wrap tog with the wrapped st. P to 4 sts after last wrapped st, working the wrap tog with the wrapped st.** Rep from ** to ** 7 more times. K to last st, pick up and k 1 st on each row from underarm, turn. P to last st, pick up and p 1 st on each row from underarm, turn. Change to the shorter circular needles and cont working in the round with these 116 sts, removing marker from shoulder and placing it at center underarm, dec 1 st on each side of marker every 4 rounds as foll: K to 3 sts before marker, ssk, k1, sl m, k1, k2tog, until 52 sts rem.

BO cuff as foll: With waste yarn, provisional CO 4 sts. With main yarn from end of Sleeve, k these 4 sts.

ROW 1 (AND ALL WS ROWS): K3, sl1, k1 from Sleeve, psso— 1 Sleeve st has been BO.

ROW 2 (AND ALL RS ROWS): K to end.

When all sts have been BO, graft 4 rem sts to 4 provisional CO sts using Kitchener st.

RIGHT SLEEVE

Carefully remove waste yarn from Back right armhole and place sts onto shorter circular needle, pm. Bring Right Front sts held on st holder under and over the loop created by the Left Front sts (see illustration on page 104), and transfer sts to shorter circular needle. Join new ball of yarn and work Right Sleeve as for Left Sleeve.

YOKE FINISHING

With a tapestry needle threaded with main yarn, sew seam on Right Front as close to the knot as possible. Rep for Left Front.

SKIRT

NOTE: The skirt is worked vertically, incorporating picked-up sts along the bottom edge selvage of the body into the work every other row.

With longer circular needle and waste yarn, using a provisional cast on, CO 130 sts.

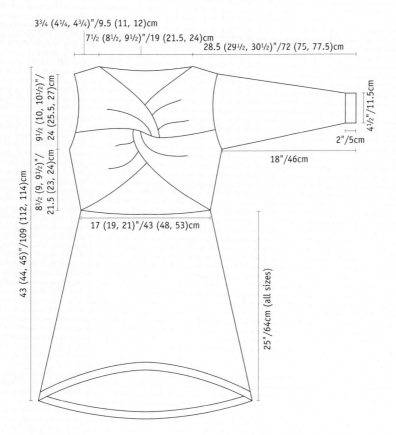

3¾ (4¼, 4¾)"/9.5 (11, 12)cm

7½ (8½, 9½)"/19 (21.5, 24)cm

28.5 (29½, 30½)"/72 (75, 77.5)cm

9½ (10, 10½)"/ 24 (25.5, 27)cm

8½ (9, 9½)"/ 21.5 (23, 24)cm

43 (44, 45)"/109 (112, 114)cm

17 (19, 21)"/43 (48, 53)cm

4½"/11.5cm

2"/5cm

18"/46cm

25"/64cm (all sizes)

With same needle and RS of back facing you, starting at the right edge, with main yarn pick up 1 st on every 2 rows along the back's edge to the left side—approx 60 sts, pm, then pick up 3 sts on every set of 4 rows along the right front toward the center knot— approx 58 sts, pm, and then starting at approx the same point on the other side of the knot, pick up another 58 sts— 3 sts on each set of 4 rows along the left front edge.

K next RS row over provisional CO sts, pm before the last 4 sts—these 4 sts will be worked in Garter st throughout. P next WS row to 1 before last st, slip last st, p first picked-up st on left needle, psso, turn—1 picked-up st has been incorporated into the skirt.

Rep these 2 rows until you reach the first marker—116 rows have been completed, 58 sts from left front have been incorporated into the skirt.

Cont working these 2 rows until you reach the next marker—116 rows have been completed, 58 sts from right front have been incorporated into the skirt.

Then, cont working these 2 rows until all picked-up sts have been incorporated—120 rows; ending with a RS row— yarn should be at the hem. Break yarn approx 3 times the length of the skirt. Carefully remove the waste yarn from the provisional CO, placing them on a spare needle, and graft the open sts using the Kitchener method.

FINISHING

Fold skirt facing to WS along fold line (4 Garter sts worked at skirt hem), and slipstitch in place with yarn threaded on a tapestry needle.

SHOULDER PLEAT:

With RS facing, place 2 pins 1"/2.5cm apart down the back from shoulder and 2 pins 1"/2.5cm apart down the front from shoulder. Fold knitted fabric along the 2nd pin toward the shoulder line, forming a large Z with the fabric. Pin fabric in place. With threaded tapestry needle, secure pleat from the collar's edge toward the sleeve for 1"/2.5cm. Join front to back shoulders for 1"/2.5cm. Secure pleats on the inside. Rep for 2nd shoulder.

Weave in ends. Wash in cold water with mild soap or shampoo, and rinse with hair conditioner. Lay flat to dry. When slightly damp, light steam-block on WS.

THIS DRESS WAS MADE WITH 21 (22, 23) skeins of Elann.com's Peruvian Collection Pure Alpaca, 100% superfine alpaca; 1.75oz/50g = 109yd/100m per skein, color #2124 Oxblood

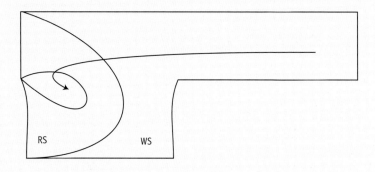

RS   WS

Knit this filigree babydoll with finely turned stitches and light, airy yarn. For a stylish, close fit, designer Melissa Wehrle smartly crafted the front to be slightly larger than the back.

lacy babydoll

DESIGN BY MELISSA WEHRLE

EXPERIENCE LEVEL

INTERMEDIATE

SIZE S (M, L, XL)

FINISHED MEASUREMENTS

BUST: 36½ (39½, 43, 46½)"/93 (100, 109, 118)cm

LENGTH: 26½ (27½, 28, 28½)"/67 (70, 71, 73)cm

materials

850 (900, 1000, 1100)yd/ 778 (823, 914, 1006)m of fingering weight mohair/ silk yarn in grey-blue

KNITTING NEEDLES:

3.5mm (size 4 U.S.) *or size to obtain gauge*

3.25mm (size 3 U.S.) straight needles

3.25mm (size 3 U.S.) circular needle 16"/41cm long

Waste yarn

Stitch holder

gauge

24 sts and 32 rows = 4"/10cm over St st using larger needles

23 sts and 32 rows = 4"/10cm over Lace St using larger needles

Always take time to check your gauge.

pattern stitches

STOCKINETTE STITCH

ROW 1 (RS): Knit.

ROW 2 (WS): Purl.

Rep rows 1 and 2 for pat.

GARTER STITCH (CIRCULAR)

RND 1: Knit.

RND 2: Purl.

Rep rnds 1 and 2 for pat.

instructions

BACK

With smaller needles and provisional cast on, CO 121 (131, 141, 151) sts.

Work 5 rows in St st, ending after completing a WS row.

NEXT ROW (RS): K1, (yo, k2tog) to last st, k1.

Work 5 more rows in St st.

Remove provisional CO, and place the live sts onto the larger needle. Using the larger needle, kn across the row, knitting 1 st from each needle tog across, forming turned-up picot hem.

Changing to Lace st (Chart A) and using larger needles, work 8 rows in pat, ending after completing a WS row.

DEC ROW (RS): K1, ssk, work to last 3 sts in pat, k2tog, k1.

Rep dec row every 10 rows 5 more times. Then rep dec row every 4 rows 8 times—93 (103, 113, 123) sts.

Change to St st and work 7 rows even.

INC ROW (RS): Kf/b, work to last 2 sts, kf/b, k1.

Rep inc row every 4 rows 7 more times—109 (119, 129, 139) sts.

Work even until Back meas 18¼ (19, 19, 19)"/46 (48, 48, 48)cm. End after completing a WS row.

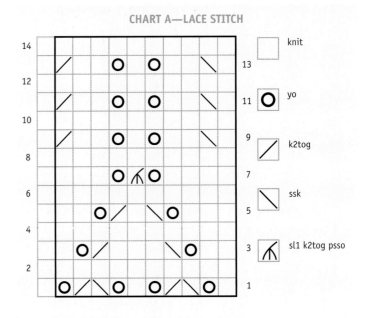

ARMHOLE SHAPING:

BO 6 (6, 7, 8) sts at beg of next 2 rows. Dec 1 st at each edge every row 4 (4, 6, 8) times, then every other row 2 (4, 4, 4) times—85 (91, 95, 99) sts.

Work even until armhole meas 7½ (7¾, 8¼, 8¾)"/19 (20, 21, 22)cm. End after completing a WS row.

NECK AND SHOULDER SHAPING:

BO 6 (6, 7, 7) sts at armhole edge, work across until there are 15 (17, 17, 19) sts on right-hand needle. Turn and place remaining sts on holder.

NEXT ROW (WS): P1, p2tog, work to end of row.

NEXT ROW (RS): BO 6 (6, 7, 7) sts at armhole edge, work to last 3 sts, k2tog, k1.

NEXT ROW: P1, p2tog, work to end of row.

BO rem 6 (8, 7, 9) sts.

Rejoin yarn and BO off center 43 (45, 47, 47) sts, work across row to end.

NEXT ROW (WS): BO 6 (6, 7, 7) sts at armhole edge, work to last 3 sts, ssp, p1.

NEXT ROW (RS): K1, ssk, work to end of row.

NEXT ROW: BO 6 (6, 7, 7) sts at armhole edge, work to last 3 sts, ssp, p1.

Work 1 row even. BO rem 6 (8, 7, 9) sts.

FRONT

With smaller needles and using provisional cast on, CO 131 (141, 151, 161) sts. Work 5 rows in St st, ending after completing a WS row.

NEXT ROW (RS): K1, (yo, k2tog) to last st, k1.

Work 5 more rows in St st.

Remove provisional CO, and place the live sts onto the larger needle. Using the larger needle, kn across the row, knitting 1 st from each needle tog across, forming turned-up picot hem.

Changing to Lace pat and using larger needles, work 8 rows in pat, ending after completing a WS row.

DEC ROW (RS): K1, ssk, work to last 3 sts in pat, k2tog, k1.

Rep dec row every 6 rows 9 more times. Then rep dec row every 4 rows 8 times—95 (105, 115, 125) sts.

Change to St st and work 7 rows even.

INC ROW (RS): Kf/b, work to last 2 sts, kf/b, k1.

Rep inc row every 6 rows 6 more times—109 (119, 129, 139) sts.

Work even until Front meas 18¼ (19, 19, 19)"/46 (48, 48, 48)cm. End after completing a WS row.

ARMHOLE SHAPING:

BO 6 (6, 7, 8) sts at beg of next 2 rows. Dec 1 st at each edge every row 4 (4, 6, 8) times, then every other row 2 (4, 4, 4) times. AT THE SAME TIME, beg neck shaping.

NECK SHAPING:

Work to 1 st before center, place center st on holder. Join 2nd ball of yarn and work to end of row. Working both sides AT THE SAME TIME, dec 1 st at each neck edge every RS row 17 (18, 18, 18) times and then every 4 rows 7 (7, 8, 8) times.

Work even until armhole meas 7½ (7¾, 8¼, 8¾)"/19 (20, 21, 22)cm. End after completing a WS row for the left shoulder. End after completing a RS row for the right shoulder.

SHAPE RIGHT SHOULDER: BO 6 (6, 7, 7) sts at beg of next 2 RS rows, then BO rem 6 (8, 7, 9) sts.

SHAPE LEFT SHOULDER: BO 6 (6, 7, 7) sts at beg of next 2 WS rows, then BO rem 6 (8, 7, 9) sts.

SLEEVES (MAKE 2)

With smaller needles and using invisible cast on, CO 54 (54, 60, 66) sts.

Work 5 rows in St st, ending after completing a WS row.

NEXT ROW (RS): K1, (yo, k2tog) to last st, k1.

Work 5 more rows in St st.

Remove provisional CO, and place the live sts onto the larger needle. Using the larger needle, k across the row, knitting 1 st from each needle tog across, forming turned-up picot hem.

INC ROW (RS): Kf/b, work to last 2 sts, kf/b, k1.

Rep inc row every 10 rows 6 (8, 8, 4) more times, then every 8 rows 1 (0, 0, 4) times—70 (72, 78, 84) sts.

Work even until Sleeve meas 11¾ (12, 12, 12¼)"/30 (31, 31, 31)cm from beg. End after completing a WS row.

CAP SHAPING:

BO 6 (6, 7, 8) sts at beg of next 2 rows. Dec 1 st at each edge every row 4 (4, 4, 6) times, every 4 rows 5 (5, 6, 6) times, every other row 5 (6, 6, 6) times, then every row 2 times. BO 2 sts at beg of next 2 rows, then 3 sts at beg of next 2 rows. BO rem 16 (16, 18, 18) sts.

FINISHING

Block pieces to measurements. Sew shoulder seams. Set in sleeves. Sew side and sleeve seams.

NECK EDGING:

With RS facing and circular needle, pick up approx 4 of every 5 sts along back neck and left front neck to holder, sl2, k1, p2sso, and then pick up 4 of every 5 sts along right front neck.

Work in Garter st for 3 rnds, working s2kp at center st on knit rnds.

Work picot BO as foll: BO 2 sts, *using cable cast on, CO 2 sts, then BO 4 sts. Place st rem on right needle back onto left needle; rep from * to end of rnd, binding off any rem sts.

THIS PROJECT WAS MADE WITH 4 (4, 5, 5) balls of Rowan's *Kidsilk Haze*, 70% super kid mohair/30% silk, .88oz/25g = 227yd/208m per ball, color #589 Majestic

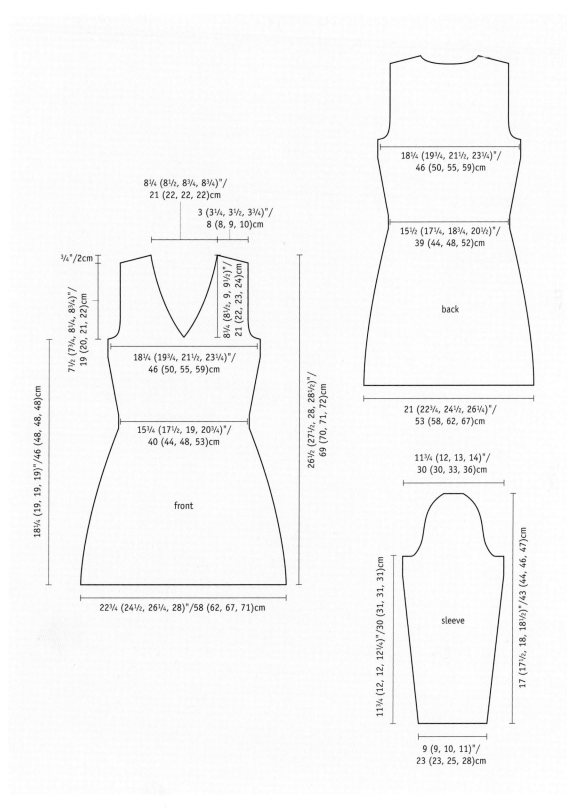

8¼ (8½, 8¾, 8¾)"/
21 (22, 22, 22)cm

3 (3¼, 3½, 3¾)"/
8 (8, 9, 10)cm

18¼ (19¾, 21½, 23¼)"/
46 (50, 55, 59)cm

15½ (17¼, 18¾, 20½)"/
39 (44, 48, 52)cm

back

¾"/2cm

8¼ (8½, 9, 9½)"/
21 (22, 23, 24)cm

7½ (7¾, 8¼, 8¾)"/
19 (20, 21, 22)cm

18¼ (19¾, 21½, 23¼)"/
46 (50, 55, 59)cm

15¾ (17½, 19, 20¾)"/
40 (44, 48, 53)cm

front

26½ (27½, 28, 28½)"/
69 (70, 71, 72)cm

18¼ (19, 19, 19)"/46 (48, 48, 48)cm

22¾ (24½, 26¼, 28)"/58 (62, 67, 71)cm

21 (22¾, 24½, 26¼)"/
53 (58, 62, 67)cm

11¾ (12, 13, 14)"/
30 (30, 33, 36)cm

sleeve

11¾ (12, 12, 12¼)"/30 (31, 31, 31)cm

17 (17½, 18, 18½)"/43 (44, 46, 47)cm

9 (9, 10, 11)"/
23 (23, 25, 28)cm

This light and airy piece is made from comfy mohair yarn but is warmer than wool.

making waves

DESIGN BY **LINDSAY OBERMEYER**

EXPERIENCE LEVEL

INTERMEDIATE

SIZE S (M, L)

FINISHED MEASUREMENTS

BUST: 41 (43, 45)"/104 (109, 114)cm

LENGTH: 26 (28, 29)"/66 (71, 74)cm

materials

1259 (1374, 1603)yd/1151 (1256, 1466)m of fingering weight mohair yarn

KNITTING NEEDLES: 2 pairs of 4mm (size 6 U.S.) *or size to obtain gauge*

Third needle of similar size for three-needle bind off

CROCHET HOOK: 2.75mm (size C-2 US)

5 buttons, ½"/1.3cm in diameter

Stitch markers

2.5yd/2.2m of ribbon for tie

Tapestry needle for sewing seams

Sewing needle and thread for sewing on buttons

gauge

20 sts and 28 rows = 4"/10cm over St st

Always take time to check your gauge.

instructions

BACK

CO 108 sts.

K 3 rows. On last row place a stitch marker every 18 sts.

Beg working Feather and Fan Stitch (Chart A).

Repeat rows 1–4 of chart until piece meas 16 (17, 17)"/41 (43, 43)cm.

NEXT ROW (RS): Beg working in St st.

Dec 1 (0, inc 1) st each edge of the next 3 WS rows—102 (108, 114) sts.

✳ **NOTE:** On right edge, work dec as a p2tog-tbl and on left edge, work dec as a p2tog.

On 7th row, work eyelets as foll: K10 (13, 16), k2tog, yo, *k8, k2tog, yo*; rep from *to* 8 more times, k10 (13, 16).

Cont working in St st until piece meas 3 (3, 4)"/8 (8, 10)cm from last lace row. End after completing a WS row.

ARMHOLE SHAPING:

BO 5 sts at beg of next 2 rows—92 (98, 104) sts rem.

Dec 1 st each side, every RS row 10 times—72 (78, 84) sts rem.

✳ **NOTE:** On right edge, work a ssk dec and on left edge, work a k2tog dec.

Work even until armhole meas 6 (7, 7)"/15 (18, 18)cm.

NECK SHAPING:

K20 (22, 25) sts, add 2nd ball of yarn, BO center (32, 34, 34) sts, k20 (22, 25).

Working both shoulders AT THE SAME TIME, BO 3 sts at neck edge once—17 (19, 22) sts rem in each shoulder.

Work even until neck meas 1"/2.5cm from neck BOs. Put shoulder sts on holder.

LEFT FRONT

CO 54 sts.

K first 3 rows. On last row place a stitch marker every 18 sts.

Begin working Feather and Fan st (Chart A).

Rep rows 1–4 of chart until piece meas 16 (17, 17)"/41 (43, 43)cm

NEXT ROW (RS): Beg working in St st.

Dec 1 (0, inc 1) st at beg of next 3 RS rows—51 (54, 57) sts.

On 7th row, work eyelets as foll: K9 (11, 13), k2tog, yo, *k8, k2tog, yo*; rep from * to * 3 times, k10 (11, 12).

Continue working in St st until piece meas 3 (3, 4)"/8 (8, 10)cm from last lace row. End after completing a WS row.

ARMHOLE SHAPING:

NEXT ROW (RS): BO 5 sts at beg of row—46 (49, 52) sts rem.

K2tog at beg of every RS row 10 times—36 (39, 42) sts rem.

Work even until armhole meas 6 (7, 7)"/15 (18, 18)cm.

End after completing a RS row.

NECK SHAPING:

NEXT ROW (WS): BO 5 (6, 6) sts at beg of row.

BO 4 sts at beg of next WS row, then BO 2 sts at beg of next 2 WS rows—23 (25, 27) sts rem.

Dec 1 st at beg of next 6 RS rows—17 (19, 22) sts rem.

Work until same length as Back. Put shoulder sts on holder.

RIGHT FRONT

Work as for back to St st section.

Dec 1 (0, inc 1) st at beg of next 3 WS rows—51 (54, 57) sts.

On 7th row, work eyelets as foll: K9 (11, 13), k2tog, yo, *k8, k2tog, yo*; rep from * to * 3 times, k10 (11, 12).

Cont working in St st until piece meas 3 (3, 4)"/8 (8, 10)cm from last lace row. End after completing a RS row.

ARMHOLE SHAPING:

NEXT ROW (WS): BO 5 sts at beg of row—46 (49, 52) sts rem.

K2tog at beg of every WS row 10 times—36 (39, 42) sts rem.

Work even until armhole meas 6 (7, 7)"/15 (18, 18)cm.

End after completing a WS row.

NECK SHAPING:

NEXT ROW (RS): BO 5 (6, 6) sts at beg of row.

BO 4 sts at beg of next WS row, then BO 2 sts at beg of next 2 WS rows—23 (25, 27) sts rem.

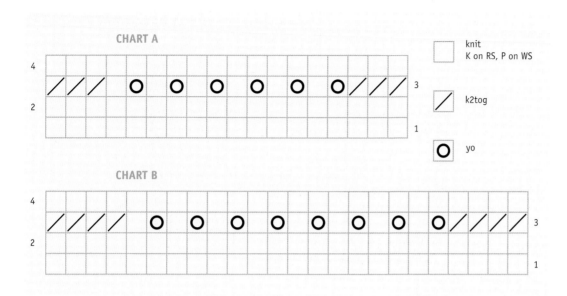

CHART A

knit
K on RS, P on WS

k2tog

yo

CHART B

K2tog at end of next 6 RS rows—17 (19, 22) sts rem.

Work until same length as Back. Put shoulder sts on holder.

JOIN SHOULDERS

Slide Right Front onto same needle as Left Front with neck edges facing.

With RS together, join shoulders with three-needle bind off.

SLEEVES (MAKE 2)

CO 48 (48, 54) sts.

K 2 rows. On the 2nd row place a stitch marker after 24 (24, 18) sts.

Begin working Feather and Fan sts as foll:

SIZES S AND M ONLY: Foll Chart A.

SIZE L ONLY: Foll Chart B.

Repeat rows 1–4 of the correct chart for your size 3 times.

SLEEVE SHAPING:

Working in St st, inc 1 st at each side at beg of every 11 (12, 17) rows until you have 60 (66, 70) sts.

Work even until Sleeve meas 19 (20, 20)"/48 (51, 51)cm.

CAP SHAPING:

BO 5 sts at beg of next 2 rows, then dec 1 st on each side every RS row 16 (20, 20) times—18 (16, 20) sts rem.

If necessary, work even until cap meas 5 (6, 6)"/13 (15, 15)cm.

BO 9 (5, 6) sts at beg of next 2 rows.

BO rem 0 (6, 8) sts.

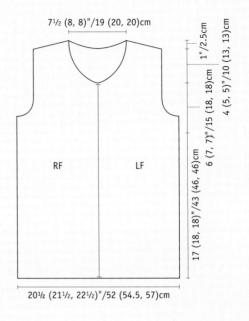

7½ (8, 8)"/19 (20, 20)cm

1"/2.5cm

6 (7, 7)"/15 (18, 18)cm

4 (5, 5)"/10 (13, 13)cm

RF   LF

17 (18, 18)"/43 (46, 46)cm

20½ (21½, 22½)"/52 (54.5, 57)cm

FINISHING

Sew in Sleeves. Sew arm and side seams.

With crochet hook, work a row of sc along the front and neck. On Left Front make 5 evenly spaced loops between top of neck edge and eyelets. Loops are made by sc, chain 8, sc in next st.

Sew on buttons across from loops.

Thread ribbon through eyelets, minding that you don't pull hard.

THIS PROJECT WAS MADE WITH 6 (6, 7) balls of Rowan's *Kidsilk Haze Hurricane*, 70% kid mohair/30% silk, .88oz/25g = 229yd/ 210m, color #632

16 (17, 17)"/41 (43, 43)cm

5 (6, 6)"/ 13 (15, 15)cm

sleeve

19 (20, 20)"/48 (51, 51)cm

2"/5cm

9½ (9½, 10½)"/24 (24, 27)cm

knitting techniques

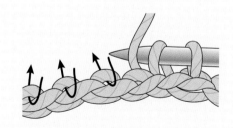

FIGURE 1

If you're a new knitter, read this over first to familiarize yourself with the techniques you'll be using. If you're an experienced knitter, check back here whenever you need a refresher on a technique used in one of the projects.

provisional cast on

A provisional cast on can be removed from the knitting, so you can work a border or another part of the garment without picking up stitches. To work a provisional cast on:

1. Using a crochet hook slightly larger than the knitting needles used in your project, make a chain about ten stitches longer than the number of stitches you need to cast on.

2. Pick up one stitch (st) through each bump on the wrong side of the chain, as shown in figure 1.

cable cast on

This technique uses two needles and is similar to creating a row of knitting.

1. Make a slip knot about 4"/10cm from the end of the yarn. This is the first stitch.

2. Knit one stitch. Leave the slip knot on the left needle, and place the new stitch back on the left needle as well. You now have two stitches on the left needle and the right needle is empty.

3. Insert the right needle between the last two stitches on the left needle and wrap the yarn as if to knit (see figure 2). Pull the yarn through.

4. Place the new stitch back on the left needle, as shown in figure 3.

Repeat steps 3 and 4 for the required number of stitches.

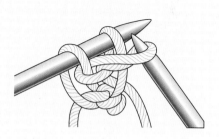

FIGURE 2

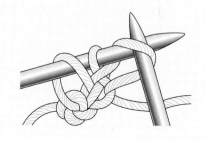

FIGURE 3

BELLY BITS preconceived notions

in the family way ❣ heavy with child

preggers ❣ gravid ❣ pea in the pod

teeming ❣ bun in the oven ❣ in bloom

picking up stitches

Sometimes knitted pieces are sewn together; at other times a new piece is knitted onto an existing piece. To work a new section that is attached to a completed section, you pick up stitches along the edge of the finished piece. This technique is often used to knit collars and neckbands on sweaters.

1. Insert the needle into the center of the stitch just inside the edge of your knitting (see figure 4).

2. Pull the yarn through. You have picked up one stitch.

3. Repeat these steps to pick up the required number of stitches (see figure 5).

FIGURE 4

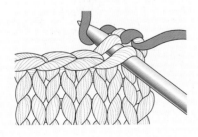

FIGURE 5

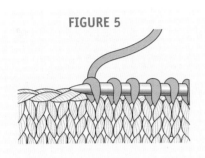

TIP: To pick up stitches along the selvedge (side edge) of a Garter stitch, insert the needle into the bumps at the end of the ridges.

SHORT ROW SHAPING

A short row is simply a row that has fewer stitches than the full piece of knitting. By knitting short rows along one side of a narrow knitted piece, you can make the piece curve. Turning in the middle of the row leaves a small hole. The hole can be eliminated by wrapping the stitch at the turning point. When instructions tell you to wrap and turn (W&T):

1. Work to the turning point.

2. Wrap: Slip the next stitch onto the right needle. Bring the yarn to the front; then slip the same stitch back to the left needle (see figure 6).

3. Turn: Turn the work so the opposite side is facing you and work the next row as instructed.

This wrap-and-turn technique creates a "float" (an extra loop of yarn) on the right side of the work. On the next complete row, you'll work back over the wrapped stitch. Knit the wrap together with the corresponding stitch on the left-hand needle to close up the holes created by the short row shaping (see figure 7).

FIGURE 6

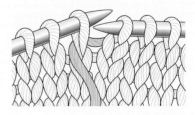

FIGURE 7

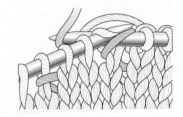

tap into your innerwear

Scratchy yarns next to extra-tender skin? No way! Wearing a soft, super-stretchy under-layer makes wearing even the softest cashmere piece so much more yummy. Support camisoles are the obvious choice for sleeveless tops; choose maternity leggings for skirts or dresses. Try a belly band for some serious support and a little extra tummy coverage.

cables

Cables are made when stitches in the knitted fabric cross over each other. Cable needles are short, double-pointed needles made especially for the purpose of knitting such patterns. They usually have a notch, ridges, or a curved section to keep the stitches from falling off while you're manipulating the cable.

To make a left-crossing cable:

1. Slip 3 stitches to the cable needle.

2. Hold the needle in front of the work (see figure 8).

3. Knit the next 3 stitches from the left needle.

4. Knit 3 stitches from the cable needle.

To make a right-crossing cable:

1. Slip 3 stitches to the cable needle.

2. Hold the needle in back of the work (see figure 9).

3. Knit the next 3 stitches from the left needle.

4. Knit 3 stitches from the cable needle.

FIGURE 8

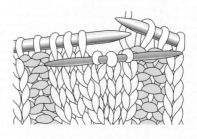

FIGURE 9

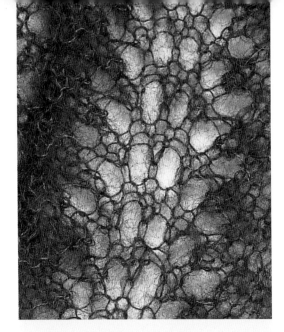

Yarn Overs for English Knitters

All yarn overs are essentially the same: you're wrapping the yarn around the needle to create a hole and add a new stitch. But English knitters must pay more attention to the position of the yarn, particularly when the yarn over falls before or after a purl stitch.

Stitch before is K, stitch after is K. Bring the yarn from the back of the knitting to the front between the needles; then wrap the yarn over the top of the right needle to the back again.

Stitch before is K, stitch after is P. Bring the yarn to the front of the work between the needles; then wrap the yarn completely around the right needle to the front of the work again.

Stitch before is P, stitch after is K. Bring the yarn from the front to the back over the right needle.

Stitch before is P, stitch after is P. Bring the yarn from the front to the back over the right needle; then wrap the yarn under the right needle to the front again.

circular knitting

Knitting in the round is used to create a seamless garment or garment piece. The technique is used frequently for making socks and neckbands, and sometimes is used for entire sweaters. When you're knitting in the round, you never turn your work, so the right side of the knitting is always facing you. To join your work:

1. Spread the stitches out on a circular needle or divide them evenly on three or four double-pointed needles, and check to make sure the cast-on edge is not twisted.

2. Join as shown in figure 10.

Lace

Lace is made by combining yarn overs with decreases. The yarn overs make holes in the knitting that are arranged to create an openwork pattern. Each yarn over adds one stitch to the knitting, so decreases are used to eliminate the extra stitches. To work a yarn over (yo):

1. Bring the yarn between the needles to the front, and then over the needle again to the back of the work to begin the next knit stitch as shown in figure 11.

2. On the next row, work the yarn over as a regular knit or purl stitch.

FIGURE 10

FIGURE 11

finishing

The way you finish your knitting makes the difference between handmade and homemade results. These techniques will help you finesse your finishing so you're proud to wear your handknits.

TUBULAR BIND OFF

The tubular bind off creates a very stretchy edge. Unlike more conventional bind off techniques, it's worked with a tapestry needle instead of knitting needles. To work a tubular bind off:

1. Cut the yarn, leaving a tail at least twice as long as the width of the knitting you want to bind off. Thread the tail onto a tapestry needle.

2. Insert the tapestry needle into the 1st stitch as if to knit and slip the stitch off the knitting needle (see figure 12).

3. Insert the tapestry needle into the 3rd stitch as if to purl and pull the yarn through (see figure 13).

4. Insert the tapestry needle into the 2nd stitch as if to purl and slip the stitch off the knitting needle (see figure 14).

5. Insert the tapestry needle into the 4th stitch, as shown in figure 15, and pull the yarn through.

The 2 stitches on the needle now count as stitches 1 and 2. Repeat steps 2–5 until all stitches are bound off (see figure 16).

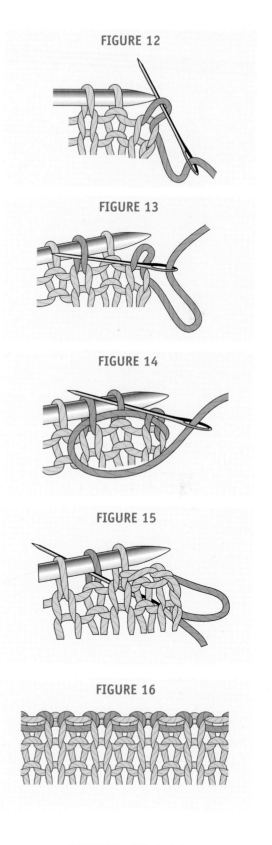

FIGURE 12

FIGURE 13

FIGURE 14

FIGURE 15

FIGURE 16

A day at the spa

Belly dancing classes

A pro nude photo session, á la Demi Moore

Aromatherapy

Jalepeño-flavored chocolates

Maternity yoga

SEWING SEAMS

There are many different ways to sew seams on knitted garments. These are the techniques used in this book.

MATTRESS STITCH

A mattress stitch seam, sewn on the right side, appears nearly invisible. It joins two pieces of knitting together, and the finished garment appears as if it were knit as one large piece. Mattress stitch is used to sew the side seams and sleeve seams on a sweater. To sew a mattress stitch seam:

1. With the right sides facing up, place the 2 pieces to be seamed on a flat surface.

2. With a tapestry needle and matching yarn, go under the bar between the 1st and 2nd stitches near the edge of one piece of knitting. Make your stitches ½ stitch (for very bulky yarn) or 1 stitch (for lighter yarn) in from the edge.

3. Repeat step 2 on the other piece.

FIGURE 17

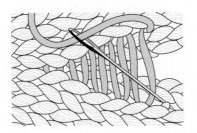

FIGURE 18

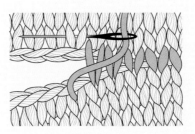

✳ **TIP:** For a quicker seam, catch two bars from each side as you make each stitch.

4. Continue to work from side to side, pulling gently on the yarn to close the seam after every few stitches (see figure 17).

END-TO-END SEAMS

End-to-end seams are used to join the cast-on and bound-off edges of knit pieces. End-to-end seams are used to sew shoulder seams on a sweater.

1. With the right sides of the fabric facing up, place the 2 pieces to be seamed on a flat surface.

2. With a tapestry needle and matching yarn, catch the knit V just inside the edge of one piece of knitting.

3. Repeat step 2 on the other piece.

4. Continue to work from side to side, pulling gently on the yarn to close the seam after each stitch (see figure 18).

✳ **TIP:** The seam should be at the same tension as your knitting and look like a row of stockinette stitches.

ARMHOLE SEAM

To sew a sleeve into an armhole, use a combination of mattress stitch and end-to-end seaming as shown in figure 19.

BACKSTITCH

A backstitch seam is often used to sew knitted pieces together, especially sewing sleeves into armholes. To work a backstitch seam:

1. With right sides together, place the pieces to be joined on a flat surface.

2. To begin the seam, take the needle around the edge stitch twice, from back to front.

3. Insert the needle into the same spot where the yarn came out from the previous stitch and back up ¼"/.5cm to the left, and pull through, as shown in figure 20.

4. Repeat step 3 until the entire seam is sewn.

OVERCAST SEAM

An overcast seam can be used to join pieces knit in different directions and to create a decorative seam. To sew an overcast seam:

1. With the right or wrong sides of the fabric facing up (as indicated in the project instructions), place the 2 pieces to be seamed on a flat surface.

2. With a tapestry needle and matching or contrasting yarn, use one smooth motion to catch the stitch on the edge of one piece of knitting and then catch a stitch on the other piece.

3. Continue along the seam, pulling gently on the yarn to close the seam after every few stitches (see figure 21).

THREE-NEEDLE BIND OFF

The three-needle bind off is used to join two pieces of knitting without sewing. It's often used to join shoulder seams on a sweater. Both pieces of knitting must have exactly the same number of stitches. To work three-needle bind off:

1. Holding the 2 pieces together on 2 needles, insert a 3rd needle as if to knit into the first stitch on the front needle and into the first stitch on the back needle. Knit these 2 stitches together, making 1 stitch (see figure 22).

2. Knit another stitch as in step 1. You now have 2 stitches on the right needle.

3. Insert the left needle into the 2nd stitch from the tip of the right needle and pass it over the fist, dropping it off the needles. One stitch remains on the right needle (see figure 23).

Repeat steps 2 and 3 until 1 stitch remains. Fasten off.

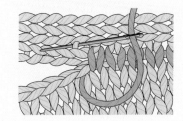

FIGURE 19

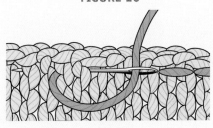

FIGURE 20

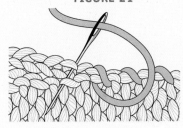

FIGURE 21

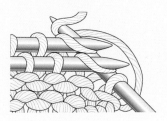

FIGURE 22

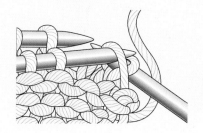

FIGURE 23

GRAFTING
(KITCHENER STITCH)

Grafting two pieces of knitting together creates an invisible join similar in appearance to the Mattress stitch (see page 120). It's used to close the toes of socks and, sometimes, to join the shoulder seams on sweaters.

To join a seam with the Kitchener stitch, first arrange the stitches over two needles with half of the stitches on each needle, and the beginning and end of the needles lining up with the sides of the knitting. Cut the yarn, leaving a tail at least

twice as long as the width of the knitting to bind off. Thread the tail onto a tapestry needle.

To prepare the 1st stitches, draw the yarn through the first stitch on the front needle as if to purl, and leave the stitch on the knitting needle. Then draw the tapestry needle through the first stitch on the back needle as if to knit, and leave the stitch on the knitting needle.

1. Draw the working yarn through the 1st stitch on the front needle as if to knit, and then slip this stitch off the knitting needle.

2. Draw the yarn through the next stitch on the front needle as if to purl, and leave this stitch on the knitting needle.

3. Draw the yarn through the 1st stitch on the back needle as if to purl, and then slip that stitch off the knitting needle.

4. Draw the yarn through the next stitch on the back needle as if to knit, and leave this stitch on the knitting needle (see figure 24).

FIGURE 24

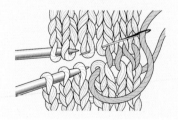

Repeat steps 1–4 until one stitch remains. Thread the yarn through the last stitch and pull tight.

SLIP STITCH
CROCHET SEAMS

Slip stitch crochet can be worked through two layers of knitting at once to create a seam that works up quickly and is easy to rip out if you make a mistake. To work a crochet seam:

1. Place the 2 pieces of knitting together with right sides facing in.

2. Insert a crochet hook into a stitch on the edge of the knitting, making sure to go through both pieces, and draw up a loop of yarn. Wrap the yarn around the hook and draw a 2nd loop through the 1st loop to secure.

3. Working from right to left, insert the crochet hook into the next stitch on the edge of the garment.

4. Pull the working yarn through to the front and through the loop of yarn on the hook. One stitch has been created and one loop remains on the hook (see figure 25).

Repeat steps 3 and 4 until the entire seam is joined. Fasten off.

HERRINGBONE STITCH

Herringbone stitch is used to sew hems because it creates a flat seam that is invisible on the right side of the work. It's also used to sew elastic into casings. To use the Herringbone stitch to encase elastic, working from left to right, sew the Herringbone stitch as shown in figures 26 and 27. To use the Herringbone stitch for a hem, working from left to right, sew the Herringbone stitch as shown in figure 28.

BLOCKING

Blocking, either by washing or steaming knitted pieces, evens out the stitches and creates a flat, smooth texture. Blocking also allows you to gently stretch the knitted pieces into shape to match the specified measurements in the project instructions.

The bands on most knitting yarns include blocking recommendations. Check these instructions before treating any yarn. Wash and block your swatch in the way you intend to treat the finished garment to make sure you like the results.

Washing a garment to relax the knitted fabric works especially well on cables and other knit-and-purl stitch patterns where pressing the item would flatten out the texture. To wash and block a garment:

FIGURE 25

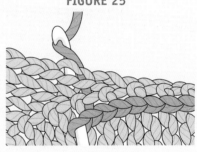

FIGURE 26

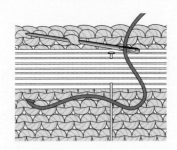

FIGURE 27

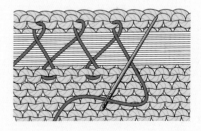

FIGURE 28

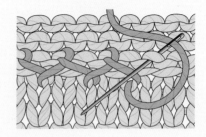

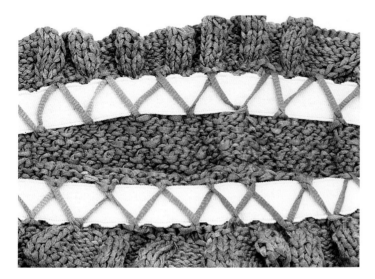

1. Soak the item in cool water until the fiber is completely saturated.

2. Roll the item in a towel and squeeze (don't wring or twist) it to remove the excess water.

3. Spread the item out on a flat surface, stretching it slightly to the correct finished measurements. If desired, used rust-proof pins to hold the item in place until it's thoroughly dry.

Steaming works well to even out the stitches on color-work and plain knitting, which may seem uneven or even sloppy before blocking. To steam a garment:

1. Wet and wring out an old towel.

2. Place the garment on a flat, padded surface and lay the towel over it.

3. Lightly press the piece through the towel, letting the steam penetrate the fibers.

4. Leave the item in place until it's thoroughly dry.

embellishment

Embellishments add flair and style to plain garments. Most embellishment techniques can be learned with a small amount of practice. If one of these techniques is new to you, try it out on your swatch before attempting it on a large project.

BEADS

Working beads into your knitting requires no special techniques. You simply string the beads onto a yarn-threaded needle as shown below, and then push a bead up to the knitting needles whenever the project instructions tell you to. To string beads onto yarn:

1. Cut a piece of thread 3 or 4 inches (7.6 to 10.2 cm) long, fold it over a piece of yarn, and thread it onto a sewing needle as shown in figure 29.

2. Push the thread through the bead; then pull the yarn through.

If you have trouble stringing your beads onto the yarn with a regular sewing needle, you may prefer using a flexible beading needle with a large eye, as shown in figure 30.

CROCHET STITCHES

Crochet stitches are often used to embellish knitting, because they work up quickly and are

FIGURE 29

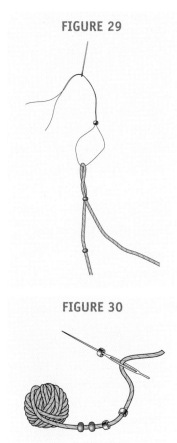

FIGURE 30

easy to rip out should you make a mistake.

SINGLE CROCHET

Single crochet (sc) is often used to create a flat edging on a piece of knitting. To work a row of single crochet on a piece of knitted fabric:

1. Insert a crochet hook into a stitch on the edge of the knitting and draw up a loop of yarn. Wrap the yarn around the hook and draw a 2nd loop through the 1st to secure.

2. Working from right to left, insert the crochet hook into the next stitch on the edge of the garment.

3. Pull the working yarn through to the front. Two loops are now on the hook.

4. Pull the working yarn through both loops on the hook. One stitch has been created and one loop remains on the hook (see figure 31).

Repeat steps 2–4 until the entire edge is covered. Fasten off.

CRAB STITCH

Crab stitch, also known as reverse single crochet, creates a decorative beaded edge. To work a row of crab stitches:

1. Insert a crochet hook into a stitch on the edge of the knitting, and draw up a loop of yarn. Wrap the yarn around the hook and draw a 2nd loop through the 1st to secure.

2. Working from left to right, insert the crochet hook into the next stitch on the edge of the knitting.

3. Pull the working yarn through to the front. Two loops are now on the hook.

4. Pull the working yarn through both loops on the hook (see figure 32). One stitch is now complete and one loop remains on the hook.

Repeat steps 2–4 until the entire edge is covered. Fasten off.

TWISTED CORD

Twisted cords make decorative belts, and they are very easy to create. To make a twisted cord:

1. Cut 2 lengths of yarn about 5 times the length of the finished cord, or the length indicated in the project instructions, and knot both ends. Attach one end over a hook or doorknob.

2. Insert a knitting needle through the other end and twist clockwise, keeping a slight tension on the cord, until the strands of yarn begin to kink if the tension is released.

3. Hold the center of the cord and place both ends together, keeping the cord taut to prevent tangling.

4. Release the center so the two halves can twist around each other, smooth out the twists so they are uniform, and then re-knot both ends, leaving an inch or two of fringe, and trim the fringe so it's even (see figure 33).

I-CORD

I-cord is a long, thin tube of knitting, usually made on three or four stitches. It's often used for belts and ties.

1. With a double-pointed needle, cast on 3 or 4 stitches as directed in the project instructions.

2. Knit all stitches. Do not turn.

3. Slide the stitches to the opposite end of the needle (see figure 34).

Repeat steps 2 and 3 for desired length. Bind off.

FIGURE 31

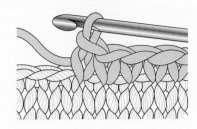

FIGURE 32

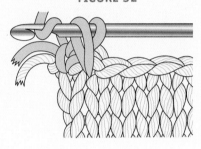

FIGURE 33

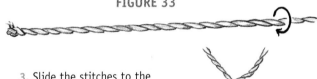

FIGURE 34

designer biographies

KATE BUCHANAN

Kate Buchanan is a knitting designer and teacher based in London. She learned to knit before she can remember and continued into her teens when a love of music tempted her away. She took up knitting again a few years ago when she stumbled across a group of women knitting in a café. Kate's passion for knitting has led her to teach and design. Her work has appeared in several knitting magazine and books. In 2005, one of her designs was a finalist for the UK Knitting Award. Kate also launched GiftedKnits, an inspiring range of knitting kits.

SAUNIELL N. CONNALLY

Sauniell Nicole Connally began her knitting career in 2001. Originally from Ohio, Sauniell's design aspirations began at age eleven. After learning to knit from her mother, she put down the needles and took up sewing instead. When she couldn't find a good fabric shop after moving to Minnesota, Sauniell's mother suggested she take up knitting. That suggestion inspired Sauniell to explore a craft that provides endless creativity in fabric and garment construction. Following two years of self-study, Sauniell began designing garments for herself and for her blog, saunshine.blogspot.com. Today, Sauniell also designs for major online and print publications.

A. L. DE SAUVETERRE

Axelle de Sauveterre is the creative force behind SauveterreDesign.com, providing custom hand-painted cashmere and other yarns for the hand-knitter. She is passionate about knitting, revels in the interplay of color and texture, and loves creating simple, elegant, and wearable clothes in the world's most luxurious fibers. She divides her time between the United States and France. See more of Axelle de Sauveterre's knitting life at two_pointy_sticks.blogspot.com.

CHER UNDERWOOD FORSBERG

Cher Underwood Forsberg knits constantly and has a houseful of semi-finished projects to prove it. A Chicago native, she recently loaded up the wagon and followed her own version of the Oregon Trail to the Pacific Northwest, settling in Portland. Cher is thrilled to have realized her dream of becoming a yarn professional, having become the Design Coordinator for Knit Picks. She blogs about her adventures in yarn, marriage, and dogs (not necessarily in that order) at tomandbel.blogspot.com.

CHRISSY GARDINER

Knitwear design is the creative outlet for otherwise full-time mommy Chrissy Gardiner. After learning to knit from her grandmother at age ten, Gardiner dabbled in fiber arts for two decades before discovering her local yarn shop. Knitting became her obsession when she discovered that wool is not always scratchy. Chrissy's designs have been published in *Cast On*, *Knitter's* and *Knitscene* magazines as well as the on-line magazines *MagKnits* and *Spun*.

She is a member of several national knitting organizations and designs for yarn companies when she's not working on her Gardiner Yarn Works line or fetching a sippy cup for an impatient child.

ANGELA HAHN

Angela Hahn learned to knit as a child and designed a number of projects before pulling aside her needles for over a decade, instead wielding needles and other sharp instruments as a small animal veterinarian. She started knitting again several years ago, and designing knitwear soon followed. Since moving with her family to Lake Como, Italy in September 2006, she has found inspiration in local scenery and fashion. Her patterns have appeared in a number of publications, including the online magazines *MagKnits* and *Knitty*, the book *Big Girl Knits II*, and *Interweave Knits* magazine. Her original patterns are available online at ahknits/typepad.com/knititude.

HELEN HAMANN

Helen Hamann's unique talents are complemented with a strong knowledge of the fashion and knitwear industry, as well as a deep understanding of alpaca fiber with all its glorious qualities. In June 2006 her first book of patterns, *Andean Inspired Knits*, was published. The book features designs inspired by ancient Peruvian textiles and tells the story of the origins of alpacas and their development through the ages. 2006 also brought the launch of Hamann's prêt-à-porter collection, Chocolate, which features luxuriously hand-knitted haute couture garments. Twice a year, Hamann takes tourist groups to Peru to explore the country's arts, culture, and textiles.

ALISON HANSEL

Alison Hansel learned to knit in 2001 while pregnant with twins and started blogging about knitting and life a year later. She had the pleasure of working on her design for this book while pregnant with her third child and is delighted that there are finally so many wonderful maternity patterns available! She has contributed patterns to www.Knitty.com and www.magknits.com as well as *Big Girl Knits* and the forthcoming *Handpainted Yarns* and she has recently published her own book of Harry Potter inspired knitting designs, *Charmed Knits*. These days you'll catch her knitting baby things at the blue blog alison.knitsmiths.us.

ASHLEY MONCRIEF

Ashley Moncrief is a self-taught knitter and designer who has been featured at www.knitty.com. She interned at the Fashion & Textile Museum in London before going on to graduate with a degree in Marketing from Texas Christian University. She is currently pursuing her passion for knitting, design, and luxury fibers. Her design philosophy focuses on narrowing the gap between fashion and comfort, while emphasizing wearability. She volunteers for several organizations, including the Botanical Gardens, an animal rescue group, and a local performing arts association. Ashley and her husband live in Texas. Visit her online at www.lushknits.com.

ELIZABETA NEDELJKOVICH-MARTONOSI

Elizabeta Nedeljkovich-Martonosi is an ex-Yugoslav doctor who came to the United States to see her daughters through college. She now practices all types of needlecraft, from sewing, knitting, and crochet to acupuncture. While she enjoys designing imaginative garments, Elizabeta's main interest is crocheted jewelry. She also speaks four languages and does work in polymer clay and metal. Elizabeta has two shops on-line: JewelLace.etsy.com and www.beta-fashions.com.

CHERYL NIAMATH

Cheryl Niamath taught herself to knit during the 2004 Summer Olympics. She comes from an artistic family, lives with her artistic husband, and works with a bunch of scientists in Vancouver, Canada. Her first pattern, Fetching, published in the www.Knitty.com Summer 2006 issue, was surprisingly popular.

LINDSAY OBERMEYER

Lindsay Obermeyer lives in Chicago, IL. Her grandmother taught her to knit and crochet. Lindsay teaches and has lectured extensively on the topics of fiber arts and needlecraft. She holds an M.F.A. from the University of Washington, an M.A.T. from National-Louis University, and a B.F.A. from the School of the Art Institute of Chicago. Her work has been shown in Boston's Museum of Fine Arts and the Milwaukee Art Museum, and can be viewed on her web site, www.lbostudio.com.

STAR ATHENA

Star Athena is a musician, writer, and artist living in Los Angeles. She learned to knit from her grandmother as a child and has been spreading the gospel ever since. A few years ago Star bought a spinning wheel, fell in love with it, and soon took home three ribbons for homespun yarn at the county fair. Star founded the annual "Tour de Fleece" spin-along to honor the Tour de France bicycle race. Star is excited about exploring original concepts in spinning and knitting, while creating useful designs. Learn about her work on her blog at keeponknittinginthefreeworld.blogspot.com.

LARA RUTH WARREN

Lara Warren loves coming up with unique knitting creations, but works full-time as an accounting clerk. She is self-taught in knitting and cannot wait to spend time in the wee hours of the night knitting away spontaneously and accidentally falling upon a new and special piece of work. Lara has a loving husband, Tres, is the mother of two amazing children, Mikaela and Samuel, and has four crazy cats. They all live in a little house in Kilgore, TX. Her other interests include playing the Irish tin whistle, sewing, painting, sculpting, jewelry making, ballet and refusing to grow up!

MELISSA WEHRLE

Melissa Wehrle's grandmother taught her how to knit when she was seven. She quickly lost interest in making Barbie dresses and put down her needles for years. Her passion was renewed when she moved to New York to study at the Fashion Institute of Technology. She graduated in 2002 and has worked as a knitwear designer ever since. Currently Melissa is a designer for a sweater manufacturer in New York City. In her free time, she designs for several small yarn companies and works part-time as the Creative Director for One Planet Yarn and Fiber. Visit her blog at neoknits.blogspot.com.

acknowledgments

Our grateful appreciation to the remarkable, inventive knitter-designers who contributed the original creations for *Expectant Little Knits*. Their unique, handmade knitted maternity wearables are more stylish than anything yet seen in stores.

Also vital to the successful production of this book were the savvy Stacey Budge, who spins, knits, and art-directs (ably assisted by Avery Johnson); editing phenom and stitch-counter Donna Drachunas; Lark stalwarts Shannon Quinn-Tucker—now serendipitously pregnant but still indefatigable—as assistant editor and Cassie Moore, super-reliable detail chaser; and the helpful folks at Yarn Paradise, the sweet little yarn shop in Asheville, North Carolina. Thanks, y'all!

—Suzanne J. E. Tourtillott